GENRES OF LITERATURE
Thematic Study Guides & Bibliographies

by

Janice J. Withington

GOOD APPLE

Editor: Lisa Trumbauer

GOOD APPLE
An Imprint of Modern Curriculum
A Division of Simon & Schuster
299 Jefferson Road, P.O. Box 480
Parsippany, NJ 07054–0480

2 3 4 5 6 7 8 9 MAL 01 00 99 98 97 96

Contents

Introduction

Welcome to *Genres of Literature*—an exciting approach to reading, writing, and language arts in the middle school. By fifth grade, most students are reading well. Therefore the primary need for middle-schoolers is to refine their reading skills and practice using them. As with any activity, whether it be physical or mental, to become better, one must practice! The lessons in this program are designed first and foremost to provide practice opportunities for students to read and enjoy literature.

What Is a Genre?

A genre is defined as a particular type of category. In literature, this applies to such categories as science fiction, animal stories, biographies, real life, nonfiction, mystery—these are all genres.

Since by middle school many students have identified a favorite type of reading, it is often difficult to tempt them to read anything else. And yet it is important that they not lock in to one genre too early—thus missing the joys of many other forms of literature. It is worth a little push to get them to try something else. By using *Genres of Literature*, students will explore a variety of genres throughout the year.

The Whole-Language Approach

This program uses a whole-language approach to the teaching of reading and writing to middle-grade students. Being literature based, the primary objective is for students *to read* and *to write.* An important piece of this program involves helping students understand how they learn (metacognition) and to develop strategies that encourage organized learning. Diagramming stories, planning a writing assignment, and applying the strategies of Bloom's Taxonomy are just a few of the ways suggested to enhance students' skills.

Reading and Writing Logs

Each student should keep two pocket folders—one for reading and one for writing. The folders will contain materials for students to use as references, such as lists, potential writing topics, assignment sheets, and so on, as well as current works in progress. In addition, students will need a spiral notebook for each subject. The **Writing Notebook** will contain all prewriting and rough drafts of pieces in progress. The second notebook will function as the **Reading Journal.**

Other Skills

Skills such as spelling and oral expression are incorporated into the reading and writing lessons rather than taught as separate subjects. Have students create their own personal word books early in the fall. Then, as they come across new words in their reading, instruct students to enter the words in their logs. Weekly spelling lists can be selected from students' individual word books.

Overall Purpose

One of the best lessons you can teach your students is that reading is fun. I hope the lessons in *Genres of Literature* open their minds to the writer's craft and help them use active reading strategies for better comprehension. Above all, I hope the genre approach will induce students to explore and discover new worlds of literature.

Reading Lessons

Getting Into the Genre

Each genre begins with a reading assignment. Students are encouraged to choose books from those you provide, from the school or public libraries or bring in their own. A bibliography follows each genre.

Structure is important when setting up reading and writing activities. Try to make due dates an integral part of each reading plan. Tell students what is expected, such as when a book should be finished, ahead of time. Encourage students to pace themselves appropriately so they will have the book read, the basic assignment done, and their projects completed.

Use a point system for evaluation. Each topic or activity earns a maximum of 5 points. This provides a quick and easy reference to see which students might be falling behind. A sample point sheet is provided on page 9.

Each class period might consist of two or more of the following activities.

- Read-aloud time (teacher reads to class)
- Sustained silent reading (students read to themselves)
- Journal time (students express thoughts in reading journals)
- Sharing and discussion time (students share with small groups or class)
- Mini-lessons (short teacher-directed lessons)

Read-Aloud Time

Since not all students will be familiar with each genre, present an introduction to the style. You might wish to share excerpts from books listed in the bibliography to high-light examples of the genre. Three books have been selected to serve as examples of the literature. Choose a book to read in whole or part to the class. You may wish to

- Challenge students to tell you which genre the book represents.
- Elicit from students a list of features prevalent to the genre.
- Encourage students to evaluate this type of literature.

If interest holds and time allows, involve students in the cross-curricular activities that follow to further enhance their appreciation of the genre.

You might also choose to read aloud from the book each day for at least fifteen minutes or as long as is needed to complete a chapter or to find a natural stopping place. This activity soon becomes a favorite for most classes. Middle-school students still love being read to. Here are some guidelines for reading aloud.

- Read the material to yourself at least once before reading it aloud.
- Ask students to clear their desks. Writing, drawing, and other activities should be set aside.
- Use a variety of "voices" to keep students' attention.
- Invite students to follow along in their personal copies of the book, if available.

Sustained Silent Reading

Sustained Silent Reading (SSR) works best when a specified time period is set—perhaps 15–40 minutes. You may wish to set a timer so everyone knows when the reading period ends. Try to schedule at least three SSR periods each week. SSR is for students to enjoy as they study genres firsthand. This can only be achieved if several rules are followed.

- Students may sit or lie on the floor if they wish—a comfortable distance from classmates.
- *Everyone* reads, including the teacher.
- No one talks or leaves their chosen spot.

Encourage students to thoroughly "get into" their books and the genre.

Reading Journals

Encourage students to jot down in their reading journals their thoughts, questions, and ideas about the literature after they have done some reading. You will find some suggested journal prompts for each genre to help guide students' writings. You may also wish to have students complete the reproducible question-and-answer sheets for their books, as well as fill in their book maps during this time.

Sharing and Discussion

This may be a whole-class or small-group activity. Set up small groups on the basis of similar topics or book titles. Try to establish specific goals at the beginning of the discussion. Groups may meet one to three times per week, depending on the unit. Encourage all students to participate. When sharing, invite each student to present the group with a quick (30 seconds or less) overview of the story. Afterward, suggest that they read aloud a compelling passage. Other members are then encouraged to ask questions or share comments on the reading, reflecting on the content.

Mini-lessons

These allow for skills instruction with the entire class, a small group, or individual students. Mini-lessons may consist of a brief lecture, a short review, a demonstration, or a group activity that reviews, reinforces, or even introduces specific reading skills. See the skills list below for some possibilities.

Skills List

Try to review, reinforce, or introduce some of the basic reading skills listed here during mini-lessons.

Elements of Literature
Authenticity
Characterization
Conflict
Mood
Plot
Point of view
Problem, conflict, challenge
Setting
Style
Theme
Time
Tone
Foreshadowing
Sequence of events
Flashback

Figurative Language
Analogy
Colloquialisms
Dialect
Idiom
Metaphor
Narrative voice
Personification
Simile
Symbolism
Alliteration
Onomatopoeia
Rhythm
Rhyme

Comprehension
Compare and contrast
Drawing conclusions
Making inferences
Predicting
Summarizing

Point System Evaluation Sheet

Genre: _____   Date: _____

Student Names	Reading Comprehension	Reading Journal	Sharing	Vocabulary	Notebook	At-Home Reading	Writing Folder	Total

Writing Lessons

Writing in a particular genre usually begins after reading the genre for a couple of weeks. Once students have read the literature, invite them to try writing. The subject matter for the writing is the student's choice. A brief brainstorming session at the beginning will allow students to offer a variety of topics and exchange ideas with their classmates. Just as in reading, due dates are important for writing. Announce them well in advance so students can pace their writing and complete the project by the assigned deadline. Explain to students the criteria on which they will be graded so they know how to concentrate their efforts. Stress that perfection is not expected on all pieces, but you *do* expect progress. Students may keep finished work in portfolios.

Begin each class period with a quick check of each student to determine what he or she plans for the day. This takes about 2–3 minutes and encourages students to set their own goals. Goals might include (but are not limited to)

- Library research
- Prewriting
- Writing and drafting
- Revising
- Conference with _____
- Editing
- Final copy

You may wish to keep a daily goal sheet on a clipboard at your desk.

Have students fill in one or two words explaining their goal for the day. If students are observed doing things other than their stated goals, quietly remind them that they are "off task." A sample goal sheet is found on page 12.

Invite students to keep lists of potential topics in their writing folders as ideas occur to them. Brainstorming sessions are helpful for topic ideas, but students should be encouraged to be alert for ideas everywhere. A conversation with a friend or relative, a personal experience, or an observation in the school lunchroom may all inspire ideas for new stories or essays. In addition, have students collect their story maps and reproducibles in their folders. These pieces will be used during the prewriting process.

Students' reading journals are another possible source of ideas to incorporate into new fiction or nonfiction stories. Encourage students to refer to their journals as they write to prompt memories and ideas about the genre. Class periods might consist of two or more of the following activities.

- Concentrated writing time
- Conferences with peers or teacher
- Editing and revising
- Publishing the final draft
- Daily language activities

Concentrated Writing Time

Set aside a specified time period of 15–40 minutes for students to write in their writing notebooks. You may wish to set a timer so everyone knows when Concentrated Writing Time (CWT) is over. Students may then switch to another activity, such as conferences, editing, or researching, or continue to write, if that is their plan for the day. Encourage students to let their thoughts flow as they write. This is the time to get their ideas on paper. It should be a creative and rewarding session.

To make CWT most profitable, try following these guidelines.

- Students should be encouraged to get comfortable.
- *Everyone* writes, including the teacher.
- Everyone stays in one spot.
- No one talks.

Conferences with Peers or Teacher

Students may wish to discuss their work with you or with their peers. Before meeting, instruct students to choose an area or two that they would like to discuss, such as spelling, punctuation, content, or another specific skill. This allows you and the students to focus your concentration rather than become overwhelmed with too many aspects of a piece of writing.

If students choose to confer with each other, they should seek peer response to the content of their writings or editing help with punctuation, spelling, form, and so on. Stress to students evaluating their peers' work that comments should be helpful and insightful. Before students meet with their classmates, instruct them to prepare three or four questions about their work that will help the peer-review process.

Questions might include:

- What type of language do you hear? (descriptive, idioms, words with double meanings)
- Does my sequence of events make sense?
- Is there anything you don't understand?
- Did I use any words incorrectly?

As students review each other's work, suggest that they present at least two *grows* and two *glows*. A *grow* is a comment that will help classmates improve their work. A *glow* is a comment recognizing something a classmate does well. Both students benefit from grows and glows as the respondent must be able to name specific skills that need improvement or represent achievement.

Daily Writing Goals

Date _____ Unit _____

Student Names	Monday	Tuesday	Wednesday	Thursday	Friday

Oral Presentations

Speaking in front of a group is a valuable skill for students to develop. A natural place in which to develop the skill is in the classroom, among friends. Although most oral presentations will be assigned in advance, you may wish to occasionally heighten the challenge by assigning some spontaneous presentations. In this case, you would omit the fourth item from the evaluation criteria. Here are some guidelines for developing public speaking skills in your students.

Requirements for Assigned Presentations

- Try to plan for two oral presentations per student per quarter. One may be spontaneous.

- One presentation should be done solo.

- Presentations should be between two and five minutes in length.

- Topics may not be repeated by the same student.

- Presentations may include visual aids, such as costumes, pictures, charts, or models.

- Post a blank schedule and invite students to sign up for the time slot they wish.

Requirements for Spontaneous Presentations

- Select students at random in whatever fashion you choose.

- Invite each presenter to select a topic from your topic supply (brainstorm these topics at the beginning of the year with your students).

- Remind students that if they are uncomfortable with their first pick, they may pick *one* more time.

- Give students one minute in which to prepare their presentations, which should last approximately two minutes.

- Try to have each student give one spontaneous presentation each quarter.

- Aim for three or four spontaneous presentations each week.

Ideas for Assigned Presentations

- Research report
- TV commercial
- Book or movie review
- Profile of famous person

- Book report
- Skit
- Demonstration
- Current events discussion

Feedback

Encourage students to provide feedback at the end of each presentation using *grows* and *glows.* A *grow* is something that will help the presenter improve his or her work. A *glow* recognizes something a student is doing well. Both *grows* and *glows* should be stated in specific terms. The following criteria may be kept in mind for evaluation purposes.

- The introduction catches and holds the audience's interest.

- The presentation is well-organized (has a distinct beginning, middle, end) and flows well.
- Correct language usage has been observed throughout.
- The presentation has been well planned and practiced.
- The presentation demonstrates originality and creativity.
- The conclusion satisfactorily ties together the important points of the presentation.

INTRODUCING THE GENRE

What better way to get students interested in reading than to have them read about children their own age? The main characters in realistic fiction could be from neighborhoods like those of your students or they could live lives totally unique to your class's experience. The story could take place in someone's backyard, in a school, or even a faraway country. But wherever the story is told, students may come to understand that they are not alone in the things they feel. By reading realistic fiction, students may learn that children all over the country—in fact, all over the globe—share thoughts, feelings, ideas, dreams, and hopes similar to their own.

- Page 16 provides summaries and suggested activities from three choice selections of realistic fiction.

- For more examples of wonderful realistic fiction, turn to page 24 for a sample bibliography.

- Strategies for reading comprehension and story analysis can be found on pages 17–18.

- Writing activities begin on page 19.

Check Out These Titles

To get students into the genre, you may wish to share excerpts from one of the following books. Or, read the entire book aloud, encouraging students to listen for the components of this genre. The books below are suggestions. Feel free to use any others you deem appropriate. If time permits, invite students to participate in the activities that follow.

Philip Hall Likes Me, I Reckon, Maybe by Bette Greene (Dell Publishing, 1974).   Beth Lambert has a problem—Philip Hall wins at everything. Could it be that she lets him win? (A Newbery Honor Book)

- Beth starts a vegetable stand to raise money. Have students work in groups to come up with their own ways to raise money. (math)
- Beth is allergic to dogs. Have students research why people have allergies. (science)
- Divide the class into groups to choose their favorite parts of the book and present their review to the class. (oral language)

Child of the Owl by Laurence Yep (HarperCollins, 1977).   Students meet a young girl from San Francisco's Chinatown who tries to find acceptance in both the Chinese and American communities.

- Research ethnic neighborhoods in their communities or in a community nearby. (social studies)
- Create a chart to compare Casey's life with their own. (self-awareness)
- Investigate the precious stones and metals that jewelry is made from. (science)

Hello, My Name Is Scrambled Eggs by Jamie Gilson (Minstrel Books, 1986).   Harvey Trumble's family has taken in a refugee family from Vietnam. Harvey wants to teach Tuan all about America, but it's difficult when Tuan sees things so differently from Harvey.

- Explore Vietnam and other countries of Asia. (social studies)
- Delve into what motivates the characters. (critical thinking)
- Debate the different things that Harvey and Quint teach Tuan. (analysis)

Name _____   Date _____

Book Title

_____

Author: _____

Who is the main character? _____

How do you feel about this person? _____

_____

Who are the other characters? _____

_____

Who's telling the story? (point of view) _____

_____

Where does the story take place? _____

When does the story take place? _____

What is the main problem/conflict in the story? _____

_____

How do the characters resolve the problem/conflict? _____

_____

What are your impressions of the story? _____

_____

_____

How do you feel about the main character once you finish reading? _____

_____

_____

Do you think something like this could really happen? Why or why not?

_____

_____

My Diary *Realistic* **Fiction**

_____   _____
Name   Date

**Think about two of the main characters. How are they alike?
How are they different? Write about them in the
diagram below.**

Character Name _____

Character Name _____

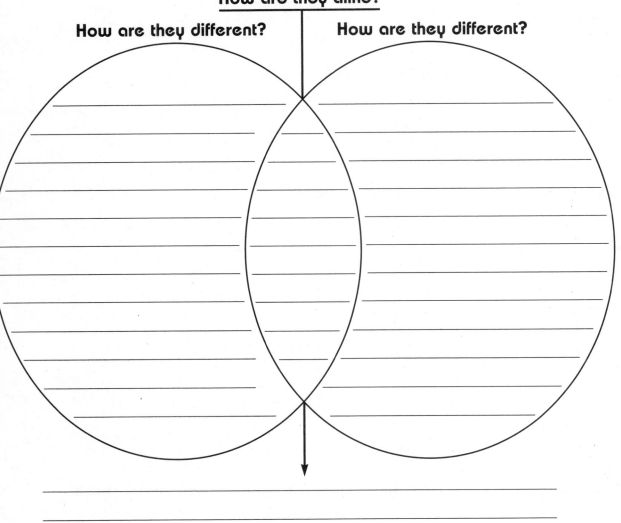

How are they alike?

How are they different?   **How are they different?**

_____
_____
_____

Journal Prompts

Invite students to write about the story you read to the class or the realistic fiction they read on their own. To get them started, suggest the following journal prompts. As students write about the literature, encourage them to think about writing a realistic-fiction piece of their own.

- Think about something that happened to the character. How would you have handled the situation?

- How does this character's life differ from yours?

- If you could retitle this book, what would you call it? Why do you think this title is appropriate?

- Why do you think the characters reacted as they did? Find an example from the story and write about it.

- Did you learn a lesson from this story? If so, what was it, and how might you use it in your own life?

- Pretend the main character visits your town. What would you show him or her?

My Diary — Realistic Fiction

_____ _____
            Name   **Date**

Think about a story you could write about events that might really happen. You might set your story in your own school or neighborhood, or challenge yourself to write about a different place you might have visited. Create a character who has a problem and write about it. End your realistic fiction with a resolution to the problem.

Answer the questions below to help organize your ideas.

Characters: Who are the main characters? _____

_____

Setting: Where will my story take place? _____

Point of View: Who will tell the story? _____

Plot: What is the main idea of the story? _____

_____

_____

Problem/Conflict: What is the problem or conflict that the character(s) need to solve?

_____

_____

_____

Other Factors: What are possible solutions to the problem?

_____

_____

_____

_____

_____

The Writing Process

Guide students as they follow these steps in the writing process.

Prewrite

Before students begin to write, have them first jot down their story ideas. Pass out the reproducible on page 20 to help students thoroughly think through their pieces. You might also suggest that they plan their stories' events by using the map on page 22. Once students have basic ideas or outlines for their stories, encourage them to start writing.

Draft

Tell students that in the draft stage, they are to let their thoughts and ideas flow onto the paper. Stress that grammar and spelling aren't that important *yet*. What *is* important is making sure they adequately relate their story ideas.

Rewrite

Now have students read their stories to see if they make sense. Explain that at this point they should check any spelling or grammar rules they were unclear about. Encourage students to exchange their stories with peers, who will read them with fresh eyes. Have peer reviewers point out anything they find confusing or lackluster. Instruct students to go back over their stories to fix any murky parts.

Proofread

Have students read over their final versions, checking for spelling and grammar errors. Again, you might let students read each other's work, commenting this time only on grammatical mistakes.

Publish

Now it is time to invite students to share their work. Post the stories on the bulletin board, and set aside time for groups of students to read each other's work. After about a week, take the stories from the board and combine them into a class short-story anthology of realistic fiction.

My Diary Realistic Fiction

_____   _____
Name   Date

To help organize your ideas, fill in the story map below. This map will help you to build the excitement of your story as your character moves toward a solution to his or her conflict or problem.

Climax
(Problem Comes to a Head)

```
_____
_____
_____
_____
```

Introduce Problem

```
_____
_____
_____
```

Resolve Problem

```
_____
_____
_____
```

Exposition
(The Story Begins)

```
_____
_____
_____
```

Denouement
(The Story Ends)

```
_____
_____
_____
```

More Writing Projects

Encourage students to practice their writing in the following ways.

- Think about the story you read. What do you think might happen next to the characters? Write about it in a story sequel. You might come up with a new problem for the character or suggest that someone new has moved into his or her neighborhood.

- Choose a scene from the story to relate in a comic strip. Divide a sheet of art paper into squares for each comic-strip frame. Then draw in the characters and write their words in speech balloons.

- Pretend you are an advice columnist. One of the characters in the story has written to you for help. Write a letter from the character explaining the problem and write a response as the advice columnist might.

- Write a journal entry for one of the characters explaining or discussing something that happened in the story.

Teacher Notes/Other _____

_____

_____

_____

_____

_____

_____

_____

_____

Bibliography

Titles that might be selected for this genre include, but are not limited to, the following.

Afternoon of the Elves by Janet Taylor Lisle (Scholastic, Inc., 1991).

And You Give Me a Pain, Elaine by Stella Pevsner (PB, 1989).

The Beast in Ms. Rooney's Room by Patricia R. Giff (Dell, 1984).

Bingo Brown and the Language of Love by Betsy Byars (Viking Children's Books, 1989).

Buddies by Barbara Parks (Avon, 1986).

The Burning Questions of Bingo Brown by Betsy Byars (Viking Children's Books, 1988).

Cay by Theodore Taylor (Doubleday, 1987).

Charlie Pippin by Candy D. Boyd (Puffin Books, 1988).

Fat Chance, Claude by Joan Lowery Nixon (Puffin Books, 1989).

The Goats by Brock Cole (Farrar, Straus, & Giroux, 1987).

Homecoming by Cynthia Voight (Macmillan Books for Young Readers, 1981).

I Want to Go Home! by Gordon Korman (Scholastic, Inc., 1991).

Just Like a Real Family by Kristi Holl (Macmillan Books for Young Readers, 1983).

Lottery Rose by Irene Hunt (Berkley Publishing Group, 1987).

Matt Gargan's Boy by Alfred Slote (HarperCollins Children's Books, 1985).

My Side of the Mountain by Jean George (Puffin Books, 1991).

Our Sixth Grade Sugar Babies by Eve Bunting (HarperCollins Children's Books, 1992).

Perfect or Not, Here I Come by Kristi Holl (Troll Associates, 1987).

The Pinballs by Betsy Byars (HarperCollins Children's Books, 1987).

Scorpions by Walter Dean Myers. (HarperCollins Children's Books, 1990).

Sixth Grade Secrets by Louis Sachar (Scholastic, Inc., 1992).

The Long Secret by Louise Fitzhugh (HarperCollins Children's Books, 1990).

The Wednesday Surprise by Eve Bunting (Houghton Mifflin, 1990).

You Shouldn't Have to Say Good-Bye by Patricia Hermes (Scholastic, Inc., 1989).

You, Me and Gracie Makes Three by Dean Marney (Scholastic, Inc., 1989).

Yours Turly, Shirley by Ann M. Martin (Scholastic, Inc., 1990).

INTRODUCING THE GENRE

Every year, one new book is selected by the American Library Association as the best in children's literature. This is a daunting task, since so many children's books are published each year. That's why Newbery winners and honor books demand special attention. They have achieved the highest recognition and students should be exposed to these excellent books. As students read, have them think about what makes the book special. Why do they think a panel of judges selected it as the best book of the year? Do they agree with the judges' decision?

- Page 26 provides summaries and suggested activities from three Newbery Medal winners.

- The bibliography on page 34 lists past Newbery winners. We've provided extra lines so you can add new winners each year.

- Strategies for reading comprehension and story analysis can be found on pages 27–28.

- Writing activities begin on page 29.

Check Out These Titles

Newbery Medal winners do not fall into any one category. They might be about history, about fantasy, or about real-life matters important to young adults. The three books below represent just a sampling of what you will find on the Newbery list.

Young Fu of the Upper Yangtze by Elizabeth Foreman Lewis (Holt, Rinehart and Winston, 1932). Students will be transported not only back in time but also to faraway China, where a young boy lives in Chunking and is apprenticed to a copper-smith. Chinese beliefs and the changing of this country are vividly portrayed.

- Create a time line of Young Fu's experiences. (critical thinking)
- Explore the history of China. (social studies)
- Read some Chinese folktales. (literature)

A Gathering of Days by Joan W. Blos (Aladdin, 1982). What was life like in New England in the 1800s? As students read this journal kept by a 13-year-old girl, they discover the joys as well as the sorrows of this time.

- Research what your community was like in the 1800s. (history)
- Create get-well cards for Cassie. (art)
- Role-play being Catherine and her friends in a scene from the story. (drama)

M.C. Higgins the Great by Virginia Hamilton (Macmillan, 1974). M.C.'s family lives in danger of a stripped mountain crashing on top of their home. How can he save his family from such peril? Could the stranger with the weird box that can capture his mother's voice be the answer? Or is it something else?

- Pretend M.C.'s mom becomes a singer. Create an album cover for her first recording. (art/writing)
- Investigate strip mining and its effects on the land. (science/ecology)
- Research who first invented the tape recorder, records, and the phonograph. (biography)

Name _____   Date _____

Book Title

_____

Author: _____

Year it won the Newbery Medal _____

Who are the main characters? _____

_____

Where and when does the story take place? (setting) _____

_____

Who's telling the story? (point of view) _____

What happens in the story? (plot) _____

_____

How does the story start? (exposition) _____

_____

What is the problem or conflict? _____

_____

What is the most exciting moment? (climax) _____

_____

How does the story end? (resolution) _____

_____

_____

What lesson is the author trying to teach us? _____

_____

Why do you think this book won the Newbery Medal? _____

_____

_____

Name _____   Date _____

Record what happens in your book by filling in the map.

Setting: Where _____

When: _____

Characters: _____

_____

At the beginning of the story: _____

_____

_____

What happens next?

_____
_____
_____
_____

What happens next?

_____
_____
_____
_____

What happens next?

_____
_____
_____

At the end of the story

_____
_____
_____
_____

Journal Prompts

Encourage students to write in their journals about the stories they read. The following prompts will get them started. As students write, suggest that they ponder why these books were considered the best new books in children's literature the years they were published.

- How do you feel about the main character? Is he or she someone you would be friends with? Why or why not?

- Place yourself in the story. What advice would you give the main character?

- If you were to visit the setting of the story, what would you see? Describe it as if seen with your own eyes.

- Pretend you are an actor and this book is being made into a movie. You have the choice of portraying any character in the story. Which character would you choose to be? Why?

- Pretend this story is told from another character's point of view. Write one incident as he or she would see it.

- This book won the Newbery Award. If the main character could win an award, which award would it be? You can make one up or present an old one.

WRITE YOUR OWN STORY

Award Winners

Name _____   Date _____

Think about what makes the book you read an award-winning title. Is it the author's style? Is it the subject? Examine and analyze what the Newbery author has achieved, and then try to write your own award-winning story.

Use the questions below to help analyze the author's craft.

What did the author choose to write about? _____

_____

Would you consider this an important topic? Why or why not? _____

_____

How would you describe the author's style? Is it simple? Descriptive? Did you find

it easy to read? _____

_____

Find five sentences that you think are good examples of the writer's style.

1. _____

2. _____

3. _____

4. _____

5. _____

Finally, do you think the author effectively conveyed the message of the story?

Explain your answer. _____

_____

_____

The Writing Process

Guide students as they follow these steps in the writing process.

Prewrite

Before they begin to write, have students first study the craft of the authors of their Newbery Medal titles, using the reproducible on page 30. Then have them outline their own story ideas by filling in the boxes on page 32. Encourage students to think their stories through clearly in the prewrite stage.

Draft

Now have students transfer their ideas into story format. Remind them that most Newbery books have a message or moral to teach. Suggest that students keep this message in mind as they write so that they don't lose the focus of the story. Stress that at this stage they should not worry so much about grammar and spelling—simply about getting their ideas down on paper.

Rewrite

Most likely, your rewrite period will take place a day or so after the drafting stage. Share with students that it is sometimes good practice to put what they have written aside for a while, then pick it up again. With fresh eyes, they may notice things that don't make sense in their plots and hear sentences that sound awkward. Encourage students to fix these problems as they rewrite.

Proofread

Once students are satisfied with their final versions, tell them to go through the stories more thoroughly now for spelling, grammar, and punctuation errors. Suggest that students consult the dictionary as well as student proofreaders for help with their final stories.

Publish

Invite volunteers to share their stories in an "Award-Winning Afternoon of Readers' Theater." You might ask them to tell which Newbery title they read and which author's craft they studied. Afterward, combine all the stories into your own Award-Winning Anthology.

STORY CHART

Name _____   Date _____

To help organize your ideas, complete the story chart below.
Refer to the chart as you write your story to recall ideas.

Setting

Characters

Plot/Problem/Conflict

Resolution

More Writing Projects

Remind students that writing takes many forms. Encourage your students to try some of the writing projects suggested below.

- Pretend that the Newbery book you read just received the award last week. Write a review of the book for your school paper, contributing your thoughts about why it should or should not have won this prestigious medal.

- Now imagine that *your* story has just won the Newbery Medal. How would you react? Write an acceptance speech to the American Library Association, thanking them for this great honor.

- Create a book jacket for either your Newbery title or the story you wrote. Remember that book-jacket flaps include a summary of the story as well as information about the author. Illustrate the book jacket, too.

- Write an ad for a major magazine that tells people why they should read this book. Include that it was a Newbery Medal winner and add some highlights from the plot. Refer to other magazine ads for design and language ideas.

Teacher Notes/Other _____

_____

_____

_____

_____

_____

_____

_____

Bibliography

Listed here are the books that have received the Newbery Medal since 1962. Be sure to add new winners to the list each year. See page 144 for winning titles of 1922–1961.

Title	Author	Year
The Bronze Bow	Elizabeth George Speare	1962
A Wrinkle in Time	Madeleine L'Engle	1963
It's Like This, Cat	Emily Neville	1964
Shadow of a Bull	Maia Wojciechowska	1965
I, Juan de Pareja	Elizabeth Borton De Trevino	1966
Up a Road Slowly	Irene Hunt	1967
From the Mixed-Up Files of Mrs. Basil E. Frankweiler	E. L. Konigsburg	1968
The High King	Lloyd Alexander	1969
Sounder	William H. Armstrong	1970
The Summer of the Swans	Betsy Byars	1971
Mrs. Frisby and the Rats of NIMH	Robert C. O'Brien	1972
Julie of the Wolves	Jean Craighead (George)	1973
The Slave Dancer	Paula Fox	1974
M.C. Higgins the Great	Virginia Hamilton	1975
The Grey King	Susan Cooper	1976
Roll of Thunder, Hear My Cry	Mildred D. Taylor	1977
Bridge to Terabithia	Katherine Paterson	1978
The Westing Game	Ellen Raskin	1979
A Gathering of Days	Joan W. Blos	1980
Jacob Have I Loved	Katherine Paterson	1981
Visit to William Blake's Inn	Nancy Willard	1982
Dicey's Song	Cynthia Voight	1983
Dear Mr. Henshaw	Beverly Cleary	1984
The Hero and the Crown	Robin McKinley	1985
Sarah, Plain and Tall	Patricia MacLachlan	1986
The Whipping Boy	Sid Fleischman	1987
Lincoln: A Photobiography	Russell Freedman	1988
Joyful Noise	Paul Fleischman	1989
Number the Stars	Joan Lowery Nixon	1990
Maniac Magee	Jerry Spinelli	1991
Shiloh	Phyllis Naylor	1992
Missing May	Cynthia Rylant	1993
The Giver	Lois Lowry	1994
_____	_____	1995
_____	_____	1996
_____	_____	1997
_____	_____	1998

INTRODUCING THE GENRE

Animal Tales

Reading books about animals is not just for young children. There are many wonderful and exciting books with animal characters written for middle-graders. Stories with animal characters enable students to experience emotions from a new perspective as well as instill a sense of sympathy and empathy.

- Page 36 provides summaries and suggested activities from three choice selections of the genre.

- On page 44 you will find a bibliography of other Animal Tale books. Feel free to add to the list.

- Strategies for reading comprehension and story analysis can be found on pages 37–38.

- Writing activities start on page 39.

Check Out These Titles

The following three books serve as prime examples of the genre. Select excerpts from one or all three to share with students. If time permits, try the suggested activities.

A Cricket in Times Square by George Selden (Farrar, Straus, & Giroux, 1960). This book revolves around Chester the musical cricket and his friends, Harry the cat and Tucker the mouse, at a newsstand in Times Square, in New York City.

- Create puppets to summarize the story. (oral language)
- Research how crickets and other insects communicate. (science)
- Explore Times Square and New York City. (social studies)

The Incredible Journey by Sheila Burnford (Bantam, 1990). Students will enjoy following three loyal pets—a Labrador retriever, a bull terrier, and a Siamese cat—as they cross 250 miles of wilderness to reach Canada.

- Make a map of the incredible journey. (geography)
- Role-play an interview with one of the animals. (drama)
- Learn about the proper way to care for a pet. (science)

Bunnicula: A Rabbit Tale of Mystery by Deborah and James Howe (Avon, 1980). Bunnicula is a favorite with many middle-schoolers. Readers join in as the household pets try to figure out who's been draining the vegetables. Could it be their new pet rabbit? Is the rabbit really a vampire?

- Write a creepy song about Bunnicula, set to a popular tune. (music)
- Research the rabbit family. (science)
- Create masks of the characters. (art)

Name _____   Date _____

Book Title
_____

Author: _____

What are the names of the animal characters? _____

_____

What types of animals are they? _____

_____

Are there any people in the story? _____ If so, what parts do they play?

_____

_____

Where do the animals live? (setting) _____

Who's telling the story? (point of view) _____

What happens to the animals? (plot) _____

_____

_____

How does the story start? (exposition) _____

_____

_____

What is the conflict or problem? _____

_____

What was the most exciting moment? (climax) _____

_____

How did the story end? (resolution) _____

_____

_____

RECORD WHAT YOU READ

Animal Tales

Name

Date

Record what happens in your book by filling in the map.

Animal Characters

Journal Prompts

Encourage students to write in their journals about the stories they read. The following prompts will get them started. Prompts will help students not only to further analyze the story but also to relate the genre to their own writings.

- If you could be one of the animals in the story you read, which would you be? Why?

- Write a short paragraph about another adventure for the animal characters.

- Pretend a new animal moves into the story neighborhood. What animal would it be and what might happen? How would the former characters react?

- Pretend you are a movie director. You are casting a new movie based on the animal story. Which actors and actresses do you think would be best for the animal characters? Explain why.

- Come up with a new name for one of the animals. Why is this name appropriate?

- If you were writing a story with animal characters, which animals would you choose? What would your story be about?

WRITE YOUR OWN STORY

Animal Tales

_____   _____
Name   **Date**

Animals make interesting story characters. When they take on human characteristics, it is called *anthropomorphism.* Animals talk, think, and act just as people might.

Create a story with animal characters. Answer the questions below to help organize your ideas.

Characters: Which animals will I use? _____

_____

Setting: Where will my animals live, and where will most of the action take place?

_____

_____

Point of View: Who will tell the story? _____

Plot: What will my animal characters be doing? _____

_____

_____

_____

Purpose: Will my story inform others about an important animal issue, or will it be

merely for entertainment? _____

Other Factors: Will people be in the story? _____

What problem might the animals need to solve? _____

_____

_____

_____

_____

The Writing Process

Guide students as they follow these steps in the writing process.

Prewrite

Suggest that students use their notes from page 40 and the story map on page 42 to record their ideas. Encourage them to write their ideas in pencil on their maps so they can easily make changes.

Draft

Instruct students to write a rough draft of their animal stories. Remind them not to worry about spelling or grammar rules yet. The important thing in the draft stage is to write down ideas before they escape. Encourage students to consider the personalities of the animals they wish to write about.

Rewrite

Encourage students to read their stories to see if they make sense. At this time, have students make corrections to grammar and spelling. Remind them to check that they have written in complete sentences and that they have conveyed events in chronological order.

Proofread

After students read their stories for final corrections, encourage them to exchange their stories with partners. Instruct partners to look for spelling and grammar mistakes and to inform the writers if any parts were unclear to them.

Publish

Have volunteers share their stories with the class. Then collect the stories into a class Animal Tales Book. Leave the book in your reading center or donate it to a younger class or the school library for others to enjoy.

Animal Tales

_____   _____
Name   **Date**

Fill in the story map below to help organize your ideas. This
will help keep events in chronological order.

What happened first?

```
_____
_____
_____
_____
```

What happened next?

```
_____
_____
_____
_____
```

What happened next?

```
_____
_____
_____
```

What happened last?

```
_____
_____
_____
_____
```

More Writing Projects

Remind students that writing takes many forms. Encourage your students to try some of the writing projects suggested below.

- Prepare a poster that diagrams the events in either the story you read or the story you wrote. Draw illustrations for key moments and label them with captions that explain the action taking place.

- Write a character sketch for one of the characters in the story you read or the one you wrote. Include such things as a physical description, attitudes, behaviors, and feelings.

- Design a print ad to "sell" your book. The ad will go in magazines and newspapers. Research some similar ads on which to model your own.

- Create a book jacket for this book. Draw the cover illustration and write a book summary. Also include a short biography of the author and jot down the publisher's information.

Teacher Notes/Other _____

_____

_____

_____

_____

_____

_____

_____

_____

Bibliography

Titles that might be selected for this genre include, but are not limited to, the following.

Agnes the Sheep by William Taylor (Scholastic, Inc., 1991).

Black Beauty by Anna Sewell (Henry Holt & Co. Inc., 1993).

Bunnicula: A Rabbit Tale of Mystery by Deborah and James Howe (Avon, 1980).

Charlotte's Web by E. B. White (HarperCollins, 1990).

Esio Trot by Roald Dahl (Puffin Books, 1992).

Howliday Inn by James Howe (Avon, 1983).

Gentle Ben by Walt Morey (Puffin Books, 1992).

I Am Leaper by Annabel Johnson (Scholastic, Inc., 1992).

Justin Morgan Had a Horse by Marguerite Henry (Macmillan Books for Young Readers, 1954).

Misty of Chincoteague by Marguerite Henry (Macmillan Books for Young Readers, 1991).

Mrs. Frisby and the Rats of NIMH by Robert C. O'Brien (Macmillan Books for Young Readers, 1986).

Rabbit Hill by Robert Lawson (Viking, 1944).

Rascal by Sterling North (Puffin Books, 1990).

Shiloh by Phyllis Reynolds Naylor (Dell, 1992).

Sounder by William H. Armstrong (HarperCollins, 1989).

Stone Fox by John Reynolds Gardiner (HarperCollins Children's Books, 1983).

Stuart Little by E. B. White (HarperCollins, 1990).

Summer of the Monkeys by Wilson Rawls (Bantam, 1992).

The Cricket in Times Square by George Selden (Dell, 1993).

The Fledgling by Jane Langton (HarperCollins Children's Books, 1981).

The Incredible Journey by Sheila Burnford (Bantam, 1990).

The Midnight Fox by Betsy Byars (Puffin Books, 1981).

The Mouse and the Motorcycle by Beverly Cleary (Avon, 1990).

The Red Pony by John Steinbeck (Viking Penguin, 1993).

The Trouble with Tuck by Theodore Taylor (Avon, 1993).

The Trumpet of the Swan by E. B. White (HarperCollins Children's Books, 1973).

The Wind in the Willows by Kenneth W. Graham, Jr. (Tor Books, 1989).

Watership Down by Richard Adams (Buccaneer Books, 1994).

INTRODUCING THE GENRE

When students think about biographies, they may envision reading about people who lived hundreds of years ago. In their minds, biographies might be synonymous with George Washington, Florence Nightingale, and Harriet Tubman. And while of course biographies of these people are excellent reading material, students should also realize that biographies can be about contemporary figures as well. In fact, if students feel more inclined to read a biography about a contemporary athlete or performer, encourage them. They just might discover that they enjoy reading biographies, which could lead them to explore others on their own.

- Page 46 provides summaries and suggested activities from three choice biographies.

- On page 54 you will find a bibliography of other biographies. Feel free to add to the list.

- Strategies for reading comprehension and story analysis can be found on pages 47–48.

- Writing activities start on page 49.

Check Out These Titles

The following three books are excellent biographies to share with the class. Select excerpts to read from each person's life. If time permits, let students complete the cross-curricular activities.

Baseball Legends: Joe DiMaggio by Marty Appel (Chelsea House, 1990). Joe DiMaggio is just one of over 30 baseball heroes featured in this series. Includes black-and-white photographs.

- Figure out how baseball statistics are calculated. (math)
- Research the location of home cities of other professional league baseball teams. (geography)
- Investigate the beginnings of baseball. (history)

Coretta Scott King by Diane Patrick. (Franklin Watts, 1991). Illustrated with black-and-white photographs, this biography chronicles the life of the Rev. Dr. Martin Luther King, Jr.'s widow.

- Role-play an interview session between a reporter and Coretta Scott King. (oral language)
- Create a time line of the civil rights movement. (history)
- Design a memorial commemorating Coretta Scott King and her contributions. (art/writing)

Bill Cosby: The Changing Black Image by Robert Rosenberg. (Millbrook Press, 1991). This biography demonstrates how the story of one person's life reflects the changing attitudes of society. Includes black-and-white photographs.

- Explore the invention of the television. (science)
- Locate old Bill Cosby shows on videotape to review. (visual literacy)
- Role-play an evening at your house with Bill Cosby as a guest. (drama)

Name _____ Date _____

Book Title

_____

Author: _____

Who is your biography about? _____

When did this person live? _____

What was this person famous for? _____

Where and when was this person born? _____

What was his or her schooling like? _____

_____

What dreams did she or he have while growing up? _____

_____

What would you consider one turning point in this person's life? _____

_____

Who were other people who helped this person achieve his or her goals? ___

_____

_____

Do you feel this person struggled much to reach his or her dreams? _____

Explain your answer. _____

_____

_____

Do you think it was a good idea to write a biography about this person? ___

Why or why not? _____

_____

_____

_____

Name _____   Date _____

Cause and Effect in the Life of

_____

Often in a person's life, one event causes something to happen,
which in turn causes something else to happen, and so on.
Record the cause-and-effect moments of this person's life
in the diagram below.

Cause   **Effect**

```
_____        _____
_____        _____
_____        _____
_____        _____
```

Cause   **Effect**

```
_____        _____
_____        _____
_____        _____
_____        _____
```

Cause   **Effect**

```
_____        _____
_____        _____
_____        _____
_____        _____
```

Journal Prompts

Encourage students to write in their journals about the biographies they read. The following prompts will get them started. Prompts such as these not only help students further analyze the biography but also help them relate the story to their own writings.

- Is this someone you would like to have grown up with? Why or why not?

- Pretend that you are this person's brother or sister. Explain how you feel about him or her.

- Do you think this person would be someone you would like as a friend? Why or why not?

- What do you think was this person's greatest accomplishment?

- Pretend you bump into this person on the sidewalk. How would you act? What would you say?

- Which teacher in school do you think would be most proud of this person? For example, a math teacher, science teacher, or gym teacher? Choose a teacher and explain your answer.

WRITE YOUR OWN STORY

Biographies

Name _____   Date _____

Think about someone who interests you. It might be an important person from history or a groundbreaking scientist. It may be someone we read about in the media today. It could even be someone who is not well-known—someone who inspires you, such as a person in your family or community.

Research the person you have chosen in order to write a biography about him or her.

Name of subject _____

Date of subject's birth _____

Place of birth/childhood _____

Description of childhood and schooling _____

_____

_____

_____

Someone who influenced this person and how the influence was felt

_____

_____

_____

Subject's dreams or ambitions _____

_____

How dreams or ambitions were achieved _____

_____

_____

_____

Subject was eventually known for _____

I am interested in this person because _____

_____

_____

WRITE YOUR OWN STORY

The Writing Process

Guide students as they follow these steps in the writing process.

Prewrite

As students research their subjects, encourage them to use the worksheet on page 50 to record their ideas. Also suggest that they jot down important moments in the person's life in chronological order using the time line on page 52.

Draft

Once students feel they have obtained enough information, invite them to start writing. Encourage them to organize their information in a pleasing way that will engage their readers. As they write, remind students to speculate on motivating events that shaped their subjects' lives. Tell students to write their ideas as they come to them.

Rewrite

Now have students reread their drafts in order to more fully shape them. Mention that students should be sure the information they present is consistent. Also have them make sure they relay the events of the persons' lives in chronological order. Finally, ask students if they feel they have painted accurate pictures of their subjects.

Proofread

Once students are satisfied with their final biographies, instruct them to proofread for spelling and grammar mistakes. Encourage them to check words they are unsure of in dictionaries or use the spell-checking function of their word processing program. Suggest that they get advice from classmates for proper punctuation and grammar techniques.

Publish

Invite students to share their biographies with the class. Encourage students, before presenting, to explain why they chose to write about their subjects. Then have students read the biographies slowly and clearly. Collect all the biographies to keep in a biography folder in your reading or social studies center.

Biographies

Name _____   Date _____

Fill in the dates on the time line below. Then write what happened in your subject's life on each important date.

Date: _____

Date: _____

Date: _____

Date: _____

Date: _____

Date: _____

More Writing Projects

Remind students that writing takes many forms. Encourage
your students to try some of the projects below.

- An autobiography is the story of someone's life told by
  that person. Imagine that the person you wrote about
  wrote his or her autobiography. Write an excerpt from it.
  Remember to write as if you were that person.

- A newspaper has decided that the person you read or
  wrote about is its person of the week. What would the
  newspaper say in a short essay about this person? Write
  a short piece for the newspaper.

- Write a fan letter to either the person you read about or
  the person you wrote about. Explain why you are writing
  and what intrigues you about this person.

- Now imagine that this person wants to thank all those
  who have written fan letters. Write a thank-you message
  from this person back to you.

Teacher Notes/Other _____

_____

_____

_____

_____

_____

_____

_____

Bibliography

Titles that might be selected for this genre include, but are not limited to, the following.

Amelia Earhart, Aviator by Nancy Shore (Chelsea House, 1987).

Arthur Ashe, Tennis Great by Ted Weissberg (Chelsea House, 1991).

Bully for You, Teddy Roosevelt by Jean Fritz (Putnam Publishing Group, 1991).

Christopher Columbus, Admiral of the Ocean Sea by Jim Haskins (Scholastic, Inc., 1991).

Jim Abbott, Against All Odds by Ellen Emerson White (Scholastic, Inc., 1990).

Jim Thorpe, Olympic Champion by Guernsey Van Riper, Jr. (Aladdin, 1986).

John Fitzgerald Kennedy: America's 35th President by Barry Denenberg (Scholastic, Inc., 1988).

Lincoln: A Photobiography by Russell Freedman (Houghton Mifflin, 1989).

Marching to Freedom: The Story of Martin Luther King, Jr. by Joyce Milton (Dell, 1987).

Martin Luther King, Jr.: Dreams for a Nation by Louise Quayle (Fawcett, 1989).

Maya Angelou, Author by Miles Shapiro (Chelsea House, 1994).

Michael Jordan by Sean Dolan (Chelsea House, 1994).

Sally Ride: Shooting for the Stars by Jane Hurwitz and Sue Hurwitz (Ballantine Books, 1989).

Story of Colin Powell & Benjamin Davis by Katherine Applegate (Dell, 1992).

Story of Sitting Bull by Lisa Eisenberg (Dell, 1991).

The Day Martin Luther King, Jr., Was Shot: A Photo History of the Civil Rights Movement by Jim Haskins (Scholastic, Inc.,1992).

The Great Little Madison by Jean Fritz (Putnam Publishing Group, 1989).

The Life & Words of Martin Luther King, Jr. by Ira Peck (Scholastic, Inc., 1991).

The Story of Laura Ingalls Wilder, Pioneer Girl by Megan Stone (Parachute Press, 1992).

The Wright Brothers: How They Invented the Airplane by Russell Freedman (Holiday, 1991).

Thurgood Marshall, Supreme Court Justice by Lisa Aldred (Chelsea House, 1990).

INTRODUCING THE GENRE

Historical Fiction

Many books for middle-grade readers are set during historic moments in time. And what better way to motivate students to learn about history then to read a fictional account of historic events? From the hardships of the Native Americans to the survivors of Vietnam, historical fiction can be enlightening and inspiring. And since most books of this genre center around or are told by a main character of your students' ages, the books become even more meaningful to them.

- Page 56 provides summaries and suggested activities from three choice selections of historical fiction.

- Check out the bibliography on page 64 for other excellent choices of historical fiction.

- Strategies for reading comprehension and story analysis begin on page 57.

- Writing activities start on page 59.

Check Out These Titles

To begin your study of historical fiction, read an exciting excerpt from one of the books below or choose one from the bibliography. Feel free to come up with your own titles as well. Do not provide an introduction to your selection. Instead, challenge students to figure out when the story takes place. You might then backtrack to read the entire book or continue reading to find out what happens. If time and interest permit, involve students in the activities that follow.

Number the Stars by Lois Lowry (Dell Publishing, 1992).   It is 1943 in Denmark. Nazi soldiers are "relocating" Jewish families, including that of Annemarie Johansen's best friend. But Annemarie is about to embark on a mission that could save her friend's life. An insightful look at Jewish persecution in World-War-II Europe.

- Explore Denmark and Copenhagen. (social studies)
- Research World War II to learn what Germany wanted to gain and how the United States intervened. (history)
- Investigate how World War II impacted life in the United States. (history)

Only Earth and Sky Last Forever by Nathaniel Benchley (HarperCollins, 1972).   This book recounts the Battle of Little Bighorn from a young Sioux warrior's point of view.

- Research Crazy Horse and other historical figures from the book.
- Locate the areas mentioned in the book on a map to see what the Native Americans were fighting for. (geography)
- Role-play interviewing key figures in the story to consider their points of view. (oral language)

The Witch of Blackbird Pond by Elizabeth George Speare (Houghton Mifflin, 1958).   Is life in Puritan Connecticut very different from life in Barbados in 1687? Kit finds out firsthand when she is accused of being a witch.

- Explore views of different religious groups in early America, such as the Puritans and the Quakers. (social studies)
- Review the colonies' dissatisfaction with England. (history)
- Compare sunny Barbados to wintry Connecticut. (geography)

STUDY GUIDE

Name _____ Date _____

Book Title

_____

Author: _____

Who is the main character? _____

During which historic time period does the character live? _____

_____

Who's telling the story? (point of view) _____

_____

Which events in the book are historical, and which are fiction? _____

_____

_____

_____

What problem does the main character face? _____

_____

_____

How does the main character resolve the problem? _____

_____

_____

What are your impressions about this period of time? Would you have liked to

have lived back then? Why or why not? _____

_____

_____

Do you think something like this could happen today? Why or why not? ___

_____

_____

Name

Date

Fill in the story events on the time line below. Place a star
next to the events that are true historical references.

The Story Begins

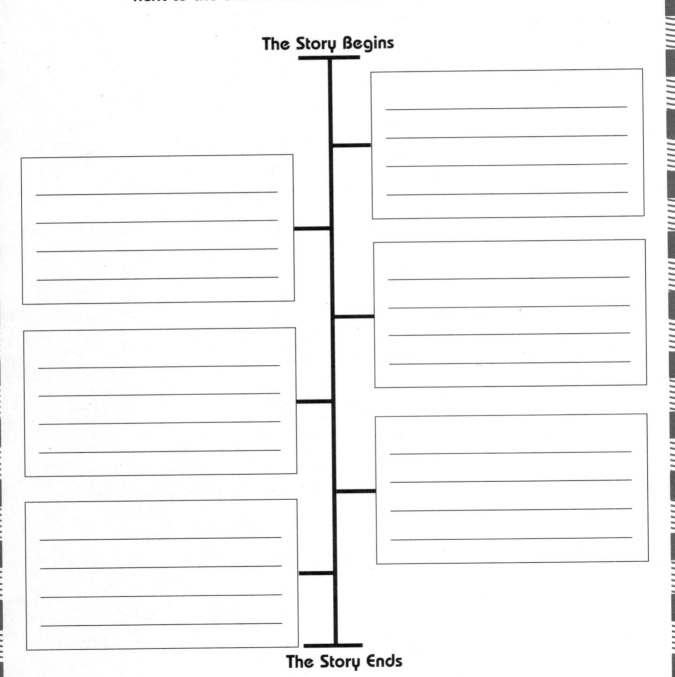

The Story Ends

Journal Prompts

Encourage students to speculate about the stories they read or heard by writing in their journals. Offer these prompts to get students started.

- What would you have done if you were faced with the challenges that the main character faced? How would you have reacted?

- Choose one of the human conflicts in the story and write a change in the event that could change the course of history.

- Describe in three sentences the time and setting of the book.

- Place yourself in the story as a friend of the main character. What advice would you give him or her about the circumstances of the story?

- What have you learned about history by reading this story?

- If you could travel back in time in a time machine, which historical period would you like to visit? Why would you choose it?

WRITE YOUR OWN STORY

Historical Fiction

_____   _____
                Name   **Date**

Is there a moment in history that particularly interests you? It might be a historic time in our country, such as the pioneer days, or it might be a time in Asian or European history when kings, emperors, and tsars ruled the land. Maybe it is as recent as 20 or 30 years ago. Put yourself in that time period and write a story about it.

Answer the questions below to help organize your ideas.

Characters: Who are the main characters? _____

_____

_____

Setting: During which historic time and in which area will my story take place?

_____

Point of View: Who will tell the story? _____

Plot: What is the main idea of the story? _____

_____

_____

Other Factors: How will history play a part in my story? _____

_____

_____

_____

Which historic figures might my character meet? _____

_____

_____

_____

The Writing Process

Guide students as they follow these steps in the writing process.

Prewrite

Because of the historic nature of the genre, you will need to set aside time for students to research their time periods in the library. Suggest that students look through encyclopedias and nonfiction books to gain necessary information. Let them use the chart on page 62 to organize their information. Once they have an understanding of what the time period was like, invite them to write down ideas for their stories, using the reproducible on page 60.

Draft

Now that students have completed the groundwork for their stories, encourage them to write. Suggest that their stories be told from either the third-person narrator point of view or from the first-person, as if the main character is telling what happened. Remind students that the most important element at this stage is to get their ideas down on paper.

Rewrite

Instruct students to read over their stories. Are they happy with how they've presented their ideas? Does the story make sense to them? Do they aptly get across the historic time period as well as the personalities of their characters? Explain that in the rewrite stage, students are to make any corrections necessary to improve and enhance the overall presentations of their stories.

Proofread

Now that the general content of their stories is satisfactory to them, instruct students to go back and check for spelling and grammar errors. After students make corrections once, encourage them to exchange papers with a classmate for further proofreading.

Publish

Invite students to share their stories with the class. You may wish to have them tape the stories and challenge the class to imagine that they are listening to a radio drama. Combine all the stories into a class book of historical fiction.

Name   Date

To help organize your research, fill in the boxes below. Use what you learn to enhance the historical nature of your story.

Who were the key people during this time?

What were homes and schools like?

What were the major industries?

How did people dress? Draw a picture.

More Writing Projects

Encourage students to practice writing using some of the following suggestions.

- Consider a historical time period or event that you read or wrote about. Write a newspaper headline and lead paragraph for it. Be sure to include the five *W*s (who, what, when, where, why/how).

- Pretend that the main character in either the story you read or the story you wrote is being interviewed by a talk-show host. What questions might the host ask and how would the character answer? Write at least ten questions and answers.

- Design and write a travel brochure about the setting and time of the story you read or wrote that would attract tourists to visit. What might visitors expect to see there?

- Write a journal entry for one of the characters explaining or expanding on something that happened in the story.

Teacher Notes/Other _____

_____

_____

_____

_____

_____

_____

_____

_____

Bibliography

Titles that might be selected for this genre include, but are not limited to, the following.

Assignment Rescue: An Autogiography by Varian Fry (Scholastic, Inc., 1993).

As the Waltz Was Ending by E. M. Butterworth (Scholastic, Inc., 1991).

Back Home by Michelle Magorian (HarperCollins Children's Books, 1992).

Blitzcat by Robert Westall (Scholastic, Inc., 1990).

Devil's Arithmetic by Jane Yolen (Puffin Books, 1990).

Daniel's Story by Carol Matas (Scholastic, Inc., 1993).

Escape from Warsaw by Ian Serraillier (Scholastic, Inc., 1970).

Faithful Elephants by Yukio Tsuchiya (Houghton Mifflin, 1988).

Friedrich by Hans Peter Richter (Peter Smith Publishing, 1992).

Good Night, Mr. Tom by Michelle Magorian (HarperCollins Children's Books, 1986).

Jacob's Rescue: A Holocaust Story by Malka Drucker and Michael Halperin (Bantam, 1993).

The Cay by Theodore Taylor (Doubleday, 1987).

The Journey Back by Johanna Reiss (HarperCollins Children's Books, 1992).

Journey Home by Yoshiko Uchida (Macmillan Books for Young Readers, 1992).

Journey to America by Sonia Levitin (Macmillan Books for Young Readers, 1993).

Number the Stars by Lois Lowry (Dell, 1992).

Place to Hide: True Stories of Holocaust Rescues by Jayne Pettit (Scholastic, Inc., 1993).

A Pocketful of Seeds by Marilyn Sachs (Puffin Books, 1994).

Rose Blanche by Roberto Innocenti (Stewart Tabori & Chang, 1991).

Snow Treasure by Marie McSwigan (Scholastic, Inc., 1986).

So Young to Die: The Story of Hannah Senesh by Candice F. Ransom (Scholastic, Inc., 1993).

Stepping on the Cracks by Mary Downing Hahn (Avon, 1992).

Summer of My German Soldier by Bette Greene (Bantam, 1984).

Timothy of the Cay by Theodore Taylor (Harcourt Brace & Co., 1993).

Twenty and Ten by Claire H. Bishop (Peter Smith Publishing, 1984).

Upon the Head of the Goat: A Childhood in Hungary, 1939–1944 by Aranka Siegel (Puffin Books, 1994).

The Upstairs Room by Johanna Reiss (HarperCollins Children's Books, 1990).

When Hitler Stole Pink Rabbit by Judith Kerr (Dell, 1987).

INTRODUCING THE GENRE

NONFICTION

Students should consider nonfiction their highway to learning about the world. Just about everything they could ever want to know can be found in books. Nonfiction may be considered dry and boring by some students—not nearly as exciting as reading about kids' adventures or following someone's life. They may feel that nonfiction books are only for research assignments. By sharing with students a variety of nonfiction books, you may help them discover that nonfiction reading can be just as rewarding as other types of literature.

- Page 66 provides summaries and suggested activities for three selected nonfiction books.

- On page 74 you will find a bibliography of other nonfiction books. Many can be found on your library shelves. Feel free to add to the list.

- Strategies for reading comprehension and story analysis can be found on pages 67–68.

- Writing activities start on page 69.

Check Out These Titles

The following three books are fun examples of nonfiction literature to share with the class. Present excerpts to demonstrate the fascinating things one can discover when reading nonfiction. If time permits, let students complete the cross-curricular activities.

The Art of Sculpture, "Voyages of Discovery" series (Scholastic, 1993). This book provides a wonderful introduction to art. Sculpture is defined as the first art form.

- Mold a statue out of clay. (art)
- Research the cultures of one of the ancient civilizations mentioned. (social studies)
- Locate on a map the places where artifacts have been discovered. (geography)

The Night Sky by Dennis Mammana (Running Press, 1989). This book provides clear yet exciting explanations for the things students see in the night sky, as well as hands-on experiments they can try on their own.

- Create and name your own constellation. (creative thinking)
- Investigate the first manned missions into space. (history)
- Research famous scientists who have made important space discoveries. (biography)

Eyewitness Books: North American Indian by David Murdoch (Alfred A. Knopf, 1995). All the books in the "Eyewitness Books" series are not only stellar resources but also terrific ways to engage students in perusing nonfiction works.

- Create a diorama of a Native American village. (art)
- Try dyeing your own white squares of cloth using berries and other natural elements. (science)
- Study the music, poetry, and legends of different Native American peoples. (music/literature)

NONFICTION

Name _____ Date _____

Book Title

_____

Author: _____

Publishing Date _____

Who or what is your book about? _____

_____

_____

Why did you decide to read this book? _____

_____

List below some topics covered in your book.

1. _____

2. _____

3. _____

4. _____

5. _____

What was the most interesting thing you learned? _____

_____

_____

Which part of the book did you find the least interesting? ___

_____

_____

Are there any questions the book didn't answer for you? What are they?

_____

_____

_____

NONFICTION IDEA WEB

NONFICTION

Name _____ Date _____

Subject of My Book

_____

What did you learn about the subject by reading this book?
Diagram what you learned in the web below. Write the main
idea in the center circle. Then list the things you
learned in the surrounding circles.

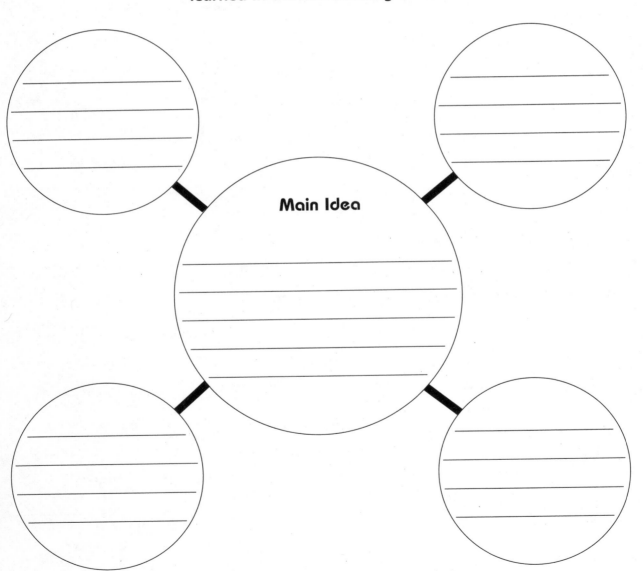

Main Idea

Journal Prompts

Encourage students to jot down the thoughts they had while reading their nonfiction books. Suggest the following prompts to encourage writing. As they write, have students consider a nonfiction topic they would like to explore.

- Before you opened this book, what did you hope to discover?

- Pretend you are a scientist or historian investigating this subject. Which new fact did you find most surprising? Why?

- You wish to present what you learned to a panel of esteemed colleagues. Write a summarizing paragraph to explain what you learned.

- Write a "blurb" that would encourage someone else to enjoy this book.

- Do you think the title of this book is appropriate? Why or why not?

- Pretend you are a book reviewer. Express your opinion of the book, your likes and dislikes, in two paragraphs. Be sure to support your opinions with examples.

- Your parents are surprised to see you reading a nonfiction book. Explain why you chose to read it in a couple of sentences.

NON**FICTION**

_____   _____
Name   **Date**

Think about something that interests you. You can choose any subject—Russian history, music, outer space, modern dance—whatever you would like to learn about.

Research your subject in order to write a nonfiction piece about it.

The subject I am going to write about is _____

_____

I am interested in this because _____

_____

_____

Here is a list of resources from which I will get information.

1. _____

2. _____

3. _____

Here are five interesting things I learned about my subject.

1. _____

2. _____

3. _____

4. _____

5. _____

I hope others learn that _____

_____

_____

_____

The Writing Process

Guide students as they follow these steps of the writing process.

Prewrite

Before students begin drafting their nonfiction pieces, encourage them to use the worksheets on pages 70 and 72 to organize their information. The worksheet on page 70 helps students locate references and main ideas. The worksheet on page 72 helps students shape their paragraphs.

Draft

Encourage students to use their notes to write drafts for their nonfiction pieces. As they write, remind students to keep the main idea and subject in focus. Explain that they should not worry about grammar or sentence structure. Drafting means getting ideas on paper.

Rewrite

Once students have completed drafts, have them set their writing aside for a while. With fresh eyes, they are sure to be more critical of their work. As students reread their drafts, encourage them to notice structural as well as factual errors. Have they strayed from the main subject or focus of the piece? Have they avoided expressing an opinion by only reciting facts they discovered? Encourage students to revise accordingly.

Proofread

When students feel pleased with their work, have them do a final check for spelling, grammar, and punctuation errors. Suggest that they exchange work with partners, who can read objectively for any problems the authors might have missed. Remind them to use the dictionary or the spell-checking function of their word processing program.

Publish

Set aside time for students to read their work to the class. Suggest that they preface their presentations with a brief explanation about why they chose their subjects. Prompt a brief discussion after each report to exchange any new or surprising ideas the nonfiction piece revealed. Combine students' writings into a nonfiction book for your reference center.

EXPLANATORY PARAGRAPHS

NONFICTION

Many nonfiction pieces are made up of explanatory paragraphs.
An explanatory paragraph has three parts.

1. introductory sentence

2. two or three sentences that support the introductory sentence

3. final sentence summarizing the paragraph.

Outline explanatory paragraphs for your nonfiction piece below.

Introductory Sentence/Main Idea

_____

_____

↓

Supporting Sentences

1. _____

_____

2. _____

_____

3. _____

_____

↓

Summarizing Sentence

_____

_____

More Writing Projects

Remind students that writing takes many forms. Encourage your students to try some of the writing projects suggested below.

- Choose a scientist or someone influential in the subject area you wrote or read about. Write a biography about that person.

- Design and write the copy for a book jacket for your nonfiction book. Remember to include a summary of the information found in the book as well as information about the author. Illustrate the cover as well.

- Entice other people to read this book by advertising it on a highway billboard. Design the billboard and then write the words to accompany it.

- Do you have any other questions about this subject? Write a letter to the author asking him or her your questions. Include how you felt about the book.

Teacher Notes/Other _____

_____

_____

_____

_____

_____

_____

_____

_____

Bibliography

Titles that might be selected for this genre include, but are not limited to, the following. (See page 144 for additional suggestions.)

A Show of Hands: Say It in Sign Language by Mary B. Sullivan & Linda Bourke (HarperCollins Children's Books, 1992).

America at War: Battles That Turned the Tide by Brian Black (Scholastic, Inc., 1992).

Ancient Greece by Robert Nicholson (Chelsea House, 1992).

B-Ball: The Team That Never Lost a Game by Ron Jones (Bantam, 1990).

Beyond Belief: Strange, True Mysteries of the Unknown by Brad Steiger (Bantam, 1992).

Born Different: Amazing Stories of Very Special People by Frederick Drimmer (Bantam, 1991).

The Boys' War: Confederate & Union Soldiers Talk about the Civil War by Jim Murphy (HM, 1993).

The Buck Stops Here: The Presidents of the United States by Alice Provensen (HarperCollins Children's Books, 1992).

Buffalo Hunt by Russell Freedman (Holiday, 1988).

Buried in Ice: The Mystery of a Lost Arctic Expedition by John Geiger & Owen Beatie (Scholastic, Inc. 1993).

Cathedral: The Story of Its Construction by David Macaulay (HM, 1973).

Children of the Wild West by Russell Freedman (HM, 1990).

The Day Pearl Harbor Was Bombed by George Sullivan (Scholastic, Inc., 1991).

Exploring the Bismarck: The Real-Life Quest to Find Hitler's Greatest Battleship by Robert D. Ballard (Scholastic, Inc., 1993).

Exploring the Titanic by Robert D. Ballard (Scholastic, Inc., 1991).

Fabulous Facts about 50 States by S. Black (Scholastic, Inc., 1991).

How the White House Really Works by George Sullivan (Scholastic, Inc., 1990).

If You Lived at the Time of the Great San Francisco Earthquake by Ellen Levine (Scholastic, Inc., 1992).

Immigrant Kids by Russell Freedman (Dutton Children's Books, 1980).

Indian Chiefs by Russell Freedman (Holiday, 1987).

Into the Mummy's Tomb: The Real-Life Discovery of Tutankhamun's Treasures by Nicholas Reeves (Scholastic, Inc., 1993).

Life in the Deserts by Lucy Baker (Scholastic, Inc., 1993).

Life in the Mountains by Catherine Bradley (Scholastic, Inc., 1993).

Life in the Polar Lands by Monica Byles (Scholastic, Inc., 1993).

The Magic School Bus Inside the Earth by Joanna Cole (Scholastic, Inc., 1989).

The Magic School Bus Inside the Human Body by Joanna Cole (Scholastic, Inc., 1992).

Our World of Mysteries: Fascinating Facts about the Planet Earth by Suzanne Lord (Scholastic, Inc., 1991).

Pedro's Journal by Pam Conrad (Scholastic, Inc., 1992).

Prairie Visions: The Life and Times of Solomon Butcher by Pam Conrad (HarperCollins Children's Books, 1994).

Pyramid by David Macaulay (HM, 1982).

INTRODUCING THE GENRE

Newspapers inspire students to read and write. With the variety of information newspapers contain, students are sure to find something they enjoy reading about. From world news to advice columns, newspapers not only inform but also provide a variety of writing formats. Point out to students that writing occurs in all phases of the media. The most obvious, of course, are magazines and print ads. But ask students to think of television—how do actors in commercials know what to say? How about news broadcasters? Someone wrote their scripts and their news reports. Writing is all around us, even though we may not see the actual printed words.

- Page 76 provides examples of different types of media that students should be encouraged to explore.

- Strategies for comprehension and analysis can be found on pages 77–78.

- The bibliography on page 84 suggests books about the media to provide additional background information.

- Writing activities begin on page 79.

Check Out These Media Options

Your exploration of the media shouldn't be limited to newspapers. As a homework assignment, ask students to look for all possible forms of writing. Here are some suggestions.

Newspapers

The following pages deal specifically with newspapers. Bring in several for students to investigate. Explain that students will be creating their own class newspaper. Encourage students to think about articles they would like to write. Here are some ideas:

- editorial
- comic strip
- sports article
- book review
- feature article
- advice column
- weather report
- local news story
- editorial cartoon
- movie/TV review
- international news story
- ads for local businesses

Magazines

Bring in several magazines and point out different topics of magazines, such as news, entertainment, sports, nature, various professions, gardening, and every hobby imaginable.

Advertisements

Encourage students to notice the print ads in magazines and newspapers. Bring in junk-mail ads you've received. Point out that highway billboards have to be written by someone, too.

Food Packages

Ask students if they have ever read a cereal box at the breakfast table. Explain that someone must create the copy that appears on these packages. Bring in boxes and cans for students to read.

Television and Radio News Broadcasts

Mention that almost all aspects of news broadcasts are written ahead of time—from news stories to sports commentaries.

Television and Radio Commercials

Someone has to write informative, clever copy for these ads. Usually it is a copywriter in an advertising agency—sometimes, the copywriter works for the company that produces the product.

news
reporting/media

Name _____   Date _____

Name of newspaper

_____

Article headline _____

Article byline (who wrote it?) _____

What is this article about? _____

_____

_____

In which section of the paper did you find this article? _____

_____

Were the Five *W*s of newspaper reporting included? _____

Who is the article about? _____

What is the article about? _____

_____

Where did the topic of the article take place? _____

_____

When did it take place? _____

Why or **how** did this thing happen? _____

_____

_____

Does this article state an opinion? _____ If yes, what is it? _____

_____

_____

What did you learn from reading this article? _____

_____

_____

_____

Name _____ Date _____

Your newspaper story is made up of many details that support a main idea. Most articles are written in the inverted pyramid style—facts and information are stated in order of importance, beginning with the headline. This enables people to scan the newspaper by reading a headline, subhead, or lead paragraph to get important points quickly. Readers continue if the topic is of interest.

Write the lead sentence of your article in the box below. Then write supporting details in the other boxes.

Lead Sentence

Supporting Details

Journal Prompts

After students have explored newspapers or other types of written media, suggest that they record their thoughts and ideas in their journals. Here are some prompts to get them started.

- How do you think the reporter/writer felt while he or she was writing this article? What makes you think that?

- Write a new headline for your article.

- If the article you read was about a person, do you think he or she will be happy with the things the reporter wrote? Why or why not?

- Pretend that you have been assigned to cover a natural disaster, such as a hurricane, snowstorm, or flood. How would you approach your interview with survivors of a disaster?

- If you could go to any country to cover the world news, which country would it be? Explain why you would like to go there.

- For which medium would you prefer to write: newspapers, magazines, print advertising, television or radio advertising, television or radio news, or catalogs? Why?

WRITE YOUR OWN NEWSPAPER STORY

news
reporting/media

Name _____ **Date** _____

Your class has the chance to publish its own newspaper. Think about a newspaper story you would like to write (or one may be assigned to you). Here are some suggestions.

- local news story
- feature article
- sports article
- comic strip
- editorial
- advice column
- weather report
- book, movie, or TV review

If you are writing a news article, jot down ideas for your article below. If you have chosen a non-news item such as a comic strip or movie review, you will use a different format.

The type of article I will write will be _____.

My article will be about _____

_____.

1. **Who** is the story about? _____

2. **What** is the story about? _____

_____

3. **Where** did the story take place? _____

4. **When** did the story take place? _____

5. **Why** or **how** did this thing happen? _____

_____

Before writing an editorial or review, complete the following.

The **topic** of my editorial will be _____.

My **opinion** is _____

_____.

Reasons for my opinion are _____

_____

_____.

80

The Writing Process

Guide students as they follow these steps in the writing process.

Prewrite

Writing newspaper articles should be constructive yet fun. Encourage students to use the worksheets on pages 80 and 82 to record ideas. Mention that if articles require research, now is the time to do it. Explain that once students have enough background information, they may begin their articles.

Draft

Before students begin, have them read several examples of the types of articles they plan to write to familiarize themselves with the proper approach and format. Then have students write their articles, using the information they gathered during the prewrite session.

Rewrite

Now have students read over their stories and make revisions. Point out that most news articles do not reflect the writer's own views but merely present the facts. Editorials and reviews present opinions of the authors *supported by facts or examples.* Instruct students to make changes that will improve their work.

Proofread

Tell students that on a newspaper staff, copy editors proofread all articles. Have pairs of students exchange articles and serve as each other's copy editors, checking for errors in spelling, punctuation, and grammar.

Publish

Arrange the class into groups according to the section they wrote for (sports, news, entertainment, and so on). You may wish to have students type their articles on word processors in a two-column format. Challenge groups to lay out their pages in a pleasing way. Suggest that students create ads for local businesses or illustrate the newspaper with "photos." Combine the pages into a class newspaper. Give it a name and distribute to other classes.

REPORTER'S NOTE-TAKING CHART

news
reporting/media

Name _____   Date _____

Many details go into writing a newspaper article.
Chart your story in the boxes below.

Headline

_____

Byline

_____

Introductory Sentence

_____

_____

Who? _____

What? _____

When? _____

Where? _____

Why or how? _____

_____

Any Opinions

_____

_____

_____

REPORTER'S NOTE-TAKING CHART

More Writing Projects

Now that students have had their taste of writing for a newspaper, invite them to write for another medium. Here are some ideas.

- Work with a group to come up with a mail-order business to sell something special, such as toys, sports equipment, and so on. Create items for your catalog and write catalog descriptions for them.

- Write a travel article about your community for a travel magazine.

- Choose an object in the class. Pretend you need to sell it in a newspaper or magazine. Write an ad for the object.

- Choose another item or product to sell and write a script to advertise it in a television commercial.

Teacher Notes/Other _____

_____

_____

_____

_____

_____

_____

_____

_____

_____

_____

_____

Bibliography

The following books all provide additional information about newspapers and the media. Encourage your students to check them out.

Behind the Headlines at a Big City Paper by Betty Lou English. (Lothrop, Lee & Shepard, 1985).

Behind the Headlines: The Story of American Newspapers by Thomas Fleming. (Walker, 1989).

Behind the Television Scene by D.X. and Barbara Fenten. (Crestwood House, 1980).

Careers for Wordsmiths by Andrew Kaplan. (Millbrook Press, 1991).

Careers in Television by Howard J. Blumenthal. (Little, Brown, 1992).

A Day in the Life of a Television News Reporter! by William Jasphersohn. (Little, Brown, 1981).

The Diary of a Paper Boy by Jean-Jacques Larrea. (Putnam, 1972).

Extra! Extra! The Who, What, Where, When, and Why of Newspapers by Linda Granfield. (Orchard Books, 1993).

Headlines and Deadlines by April Koral. (Julian Messner, 1981).

I Can Be a Reporter by Christine Maloney Fitz-Gerald. (Children's Press, 1986).

In the Newsroom by April Koral. (Franklin Watts, 1989).

Magazine: Behind the Scenes at "Sports Illustrated" by William Jasphersohn. (Little, Brown, 1983).

The News Media by Ruth and Mike Wolverton. (Franklin Watts, 1981).

Nineteenth Century America: The Newspapers by Leonard Everett Fisher. (Holiday House, 1981).

Publishing Careers: Magazines and Books by Charles Paul May. (Franklin Watts, 1978).

TV and Radio Careers by D.X. Fenten. (Franklin Watts, 1976).

INTRODUCING THE GENRE

Messages written in secret code . . . clues leading to more clues . . . a brain-twisting puzzle that appears to have no end. Who doesn't love a good mystery? And student-aged characters who solve mysteries are an exciting read. But mysteries also serve another purpose. They encourage students to use essential critical-thinking skills. Students will find themselves, consciously or subconsciously, trying to solve the mystery. Where do the clues lead? What is the importance of the secret code? Mysteries call on students to sort out plots, employ logistics, make predictions, and analyze characters. What more could teachers ask?

- On page 86 you will find suggestions for three mystery books that will convey the nature of the genre.

- The bibliography on page 94 suggests mystery books for students to read on their own.

- Strategies for reading comprehension and story analysis can be found on pages 87–88.

- Writing activities begin on page 89.

Check Out These Titles

Share excerpts from the following titles to get students intrigued with mysteries—if they aren't already. In addition to the classic titles listed below, many current series are appropriate, such as the updated Hardy Boys and Nancy Drew stories. Don't shy away from letting your students read these books. Not only do they have the proper "who-done-it?" format, but they also get students to *read*.

From the Mixed-Up Files of Mrs. Basil E. Frankweiler by E. L. Konigsberg (Atheneum, 1967).   Students are sure to enjoy Claudia's novel idea to run away and live at the Metropolitan Museum of Art in New York City.

- Create a floor plan of your school, based on the floor plan of the museum in the book. (mapping)
- Draw up a brochure for a museum in or near your area. (art/travel)
- Research a piece of art and its artist. (humanities)

The Egypt Game by Zilpha Keatley Snyder (Macmillan, 1967). When April and Melanie design their own game, they never dream that it will lead to a true criminal investigation.

- Create your own board game based on a story you read. (art)
- Research what ancient Egypt was like and turn your findings into a mobile. (history)
- Investigate what it takes to be an archaeologist and write a paragraph stating whether or not you'd like to be one. (science)

Encyclopedia Brown by Donald J. Sobol (Lodestar/Morrow, 1963). Even though Leroy "Encyclopedia" Brown's father is the chief of police, it is usually Encyclopedia who helps solve the town of Idaville's mysteries.

- Create a medal or award to honor Encyclopedia Brown. (art)
- Act out one of the mysteries that Encyclopedia had to solve. (drama)
- Debate whether or not Encyclopedia truly has a detective's mind. (oral language)

Mystery

_____   _____
Name   Date

Book Title

_____

Author: _____

Who is the detective/mystery solver? _____

What is the mystery that needs to be solved? _____

_____

_____

Who are the detective's assistants, if any? _____

_____

Who are the mysterious characters? _____

_____

List some clues that help solve the mystery. _____

_____

_____

_____

A "red herring" is a clue that is added to throw the detective and the reader off
track. It's like a fake clue. List any red herrings in this mystery. _____

_____

_____

_____

How is the mystery solved? _____

_____

_____

_____

Name _____   Date _____

What is the mystery that the main character is trying to solve?
Write about it in the center box. Write the clues that lead to
the final solution in the circles around the box. Then
write the solution in the bottom box.

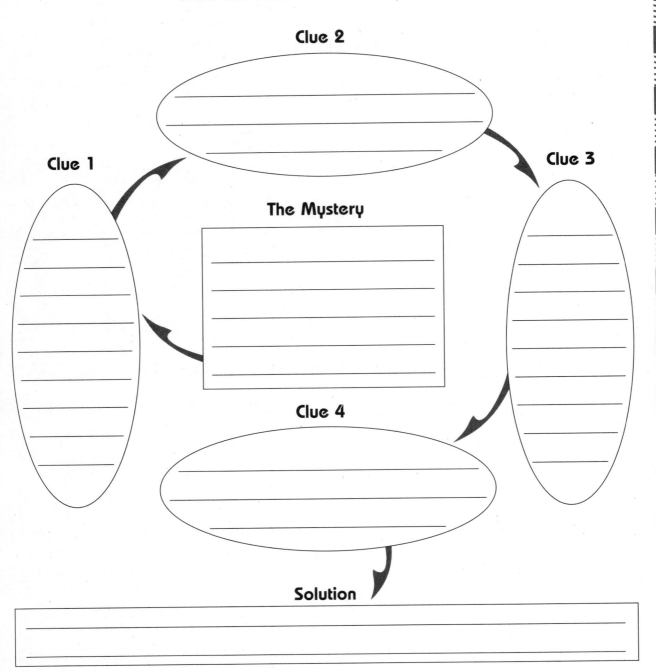

Journal Prompts

Encourage students to write in their journals about the mysteries they read. The following prompts will get them started. Suggest that they keep in mind the different important aspects of a mystery in order to write their own.

- Solving this mystery is big news. Come up with three newspaper headlines that summarize what happened.

- Write about how the main character felt before, during, and after the mystery.

- You are a reporter. What would you like to ask the detective or mystery solver? Come up with five questions.

- Plans are in the works to make a TV show based on the main character and other mysteries he or she might solve. What could the show be called? Explain your answer.

- Come up with another mystery for the main character to solve.

- Would you like to have the main character as a friend? Why or why not?

_____   _____
Name   **Date**

Is there something mysterious that might happen in your
school or community? Write a mystery story of your own.
Here's a hint to get you started—figure out what the mystery is
and then work backward to cover up the mystery's tracks.

Write ideas for your mystery below.

Main Character: Who is my detective? _____

_____

Setting: Where and when does the main action of my mystery take place? ____

_____

_____

Point of View: Who is telling us about the mystery? _____

_____

Plot: What is the mystery that has to be solved? _____

_____

_____

Outcome: What is the solution to the mystery? _____

_____

_____

Other Factors: Who will the "villains" be? _____

_____

Who will the helpers be? _____

_____

_____

The Writing Process

Guide students as they follow these steps in the writing process.

Prewrite

A great deal of planning goes into the writing of a mystery. It may help to plan the ending or solution in advance. All the details of the story need to dovetail with this ending. The worksheet on page 92 has been set up to help students plot their stories *backward.* This way they can outline the events that lead up to the solution in chronological order.

Draft

Once students have a firm plot line in mind, invite them to start writing. Remind them that in the draft stage, the most important thing is to get their ideas down on paper. Later they can go back and check for spelling and punctuation.

Rewrite

Ask students to read their stories. Do their mysteries make sense? Are they suspenseful? Do the events leading up to the solutions provide enough clues to solve the mysteries? Have they left a few unanswered questions so the endings are not too obvious? Are they happy with their detectives? Have students rework their stories until they are satisfied.

Proofread

Have students read their stories again, paying special attention to spelling, punctuation, and grammar. Encourage students to exchange their stories with classmates and check for errors.

Publish

Select some mysteries that you feel are well written. Dim the lights in your classroom. Ask students to close their eyes and pretend that they are listening to a radio mystery drama, as people once used to do. Then read the mysteries. Before the ending of each mystery, turn on the lights and challenge students to solve it.

_____   _____
Name   Date

Write the solution to your mystery in the top box. Then think about the clues that will lead the detective to solve the mystery. What is the final, deciding clue? What clue comes before it? What is the first clue the detective stumbles upon? Write your ideas in the boxes below.

Mystery Solution

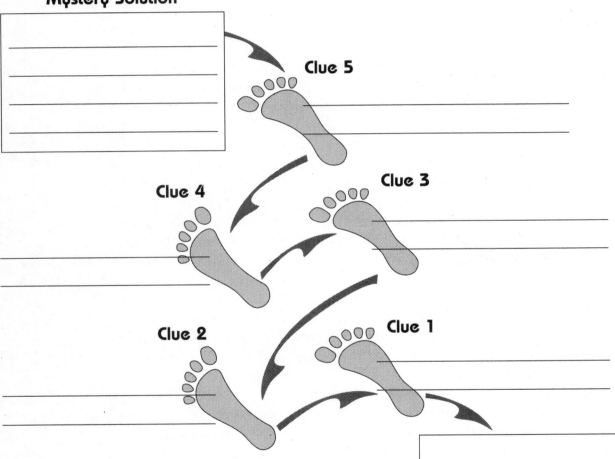

Clue 5

Clue 4

Clue 3

Clue 2

Clue 1

What's the mystery?

More Writing Projects

Remind students that writing takes many forms. Encourage your students to stretch their writing skills by trying the following.

- Create a "Wanted" poster for the villain of the mystery you read or the mystery you wrote.

- Write a thank-you letter from the people of the community thanking the detective for solving the mystery.

- Write a short biography about the mystery solver. Include where he or she was born, details about his or her family, the school she or he attends, and any special interests (aside from detective work).

- Write the letters of the detective's name vertically down one side of a sheet of paper. For each letter, start a sentence that describes him or her.

- Pretend your detective is a performer. What are the detective's "Greatest Hits"? Write and design an album cover featuring your detective.

Teacher Notes/Other _____

_____

_____

_____

_____

_____

_____

_____

_____

Bibliography

Encourage students to read a variety of mysteries. Here are some they might enjoy.

The Arm of the Starfish by Madeleine L'Engle (Dell, 1980).

The Court of the Stone Children by Eleanor Cameron (Puffin Books, 1990).

Deadly Promise by Joan Lowery Nixon (Bantam, 1993).

Dollhouse Murders by Betty Ren Wright (Scholastic, Inc., 1985).

The Face on the Milk Carton by Caroline B. Cooney (Bantam, 1990).

The Ghost in the Third Row by Bruce Coville (Bantam, 1987).

Harriet the Spy by Louise Fitzhugh (HarperCollins Children's Books, 1990).

Hideout by Eve Bunting (Harcourt Brace & Co., 1993).

Is Anybody There? by Eve Bunting (HarperCollins Children's Books, 1990).

The Letter, the Witch, and the Ring by John Bellairs (Puffin Books, 1993).

The Long Secret by Louise Fitzhugh (HarperCollins Children's Books, 1990).

Miracle at Clement's Pond by Patricia Pendergraft (Putnam Publishing Group, 1987).

The Mysterious Disappearance of Leon (I Mean Noel) by Ellen Raskin (Puffin Books, 1989).

Mystery Hideout by Ken Follett (Scholastic, Inc., 1991).

Mystery at Snowshoe Mountain Lodge by Lisa Eisenberg (Dial Books for Young Readers, 1987).

Mystery on October Road by Allison C. Herzig and Jane Lawrence Mali (Puffin Books, 1993).

My Teacher Is an Alien by Bruce Coville (PB, 1989).

Our Teacher Is Missing by Mary Francis Shura (Scholastic, Inc., 1993).

Sam, the Cat Detective by Linda Stewart (Scholastic, Inc., 1993).

Trouble at Marsh Harbor by Susan Sharpe (Puffin Books, 1991).

Voices After Midnight by Richard Peck (Yearling Classics, 1990).

Wake Me at Midnight by Barthe DeClements (Puffin Books, 1993).

The Westing Game by Ellen Raskin (Puffin Books, 1992).

When the Dolls Woke by Marjorie Filley Stover (Albert Whitman & Co., 1985).

Who Stole the Wizard of Oz? by Avi (Random House Books for Young Readers, 1990).

INTRODUCING THE GENRE

This genre is a particularly exciting one for students to explore. As they read, students are transported not only through time but also to different places and realms. These books may take place in the future or on imagined faraway planets. Or they might take place in a different place altogether—a place full of magic and mystery— perhaps even in a universe parallel to earth. The themes and morals ingeniously woven into these tales are also interesting for students to unravel and study.

- Page 96 suggests three excellent choices in the genre to share with the class, as well as activities if time permits.

- On page 104 you will find a bibliography of other Science Fiction and Fantasy books. Feel free to add to the list.

- Strategies for reading comprehension and story analysis can be found on pages 97–98.

- Writing activities start on page 99.

Check Out These Titles

The books below are prime examples of the Science Fiction/ Fantasy genre. Read excerpts to provide students with a feel for these books. If time and interest hold, involve the class in the activities that follow.

Enchantress from the Stars by Sylvia Engdahl (Peter Smith, 1991). This story takes place on a distant planet, Andrecia. When visitors from another planet land there, they feel the inhabitants are inferior and set out to take over their world. But travelers from a third planet, which include the heroine Elana, intervene.

- Study the environmental effects of current-day mining practices. (ecology)
- Research recent discoveries in space. (science)
- Debate the issues presented in the book. (critical thinking)

The Dark Is Rising by Susan Cooper (Macmillan, 1973). This book is part of an award-winning series. On his 11th birthday, Will Stanton discovers that he has a secret destiny—to protect the world from the evil forces of the Dark. All the books in the series deal with good versus evil, mythical beings, and magical elements.

- Create a radio drama of the story events. (oral language)
- Investigate how crystals form. (science)
- Explore England, where Will is from. (geography)

The Book of Three by Lloyd Alexander (Atheneum, 1964). This is the first book about the mythical land of Prydain. It follows Taran and his dreams of discovering not only who he is but also who he will become. Along the way, Taran meets many amazing beings, both friends and enemies.

- Make a map of Taran's world. (geography)
- Explore Wales, the country that inspired the author to write the story. (social studies)
- Read other tales from Wales, particularly the legend of King Arthur. (literature)

Name _____   Date _____

Book Title

_____

Author: _____

Who is the main character? _____

What is his or her goal or purpose? _____

_____

Where and when does the story take place? _____

_____

Who are the other main characters? _____

_____

Describe any magical elements in the story. _____

_____

Who's telling the story? (point of view) _____

_____

How does the main character set about achieving the goals? _____

_____

_____

_____

What obstacles does he or she face? _____

_____

_____

_____

What is the most exciting moment? (climax) _____

_____

_____

Name _____   Date _____

Record who the characters are and how they help the main character by filling in the character web below.

Contributions

Contributions

Character Name

Character Name

The main character is

Contributions

Character Name

Character Name

Contributions

Journal Prompts

The following prompts are based on Bloom's Taxonomy. Use them not only to encourage and enhance students' writing but also to gain knowledge of their understanding of the literature.

- How would you describe the setting? Is it a place you would like to visit? Describe the setting and explain how you feel about it. (comprehension)

- Summarize the plot in six sentences. Make sure you write your sentences in chronological order. (application)

- Which elements make this story a tale of fantasy or science fiction? Could this story really happen? Why or why not? (analysis)

- Add another character to the story. What kind of creature is it? Is it magical? Is it a normal child? What part will it play in the story? (synthesis)

- How do you feel about this story? Did you like reading about something that takes place in an imaginary world? Why or why not? Write your opinions on reading fantasy or science fiction. (evaluation)

Name _____   Date _____

If you could make up a world—any world at all—what would it be like? This is the kind of thing fantasy and science-fiction writers think about all the time. Would your world have magical elements? Would it be in a distant galaxy? Have a different time structure than ours? Try writing a science fiction or fantasy story. Use the questions below to get you started.

Setting: Will my story take place on a distant planet or in a magical world? _____

What will this world be like? _____

_____

Main Character: Who will my main character be? _____

_____

Will my character have any special powers? _____

_____

Other Characters: Who will the other characters be? _____

_____

What special abilities will these characters have, if any? _____

_____

_____

Plot: What will the characters strive to do? _____

_____

_____

Other Factors: Forces of Good _____

Forces of Evil _____

The Writing Process

Guide students as they follow these steps in the writing process.

Prewrite

Before they begin to write, instruct students to plan their stories by answering the questions found on page 100 and by filling in the diagram found on page 102. Tell students that this is the stage to brainstorm all possible ideas. They may hang onto those they find most interesting and toss aside those they find less compelling.

Draft

Using their thoughts from the worksheet and diagram, encourage students to write their stories, using descriptive language that conveys what their fantasy worlds and characters are like. As they write their drafts, encourage students to keep in mind the goals their characters are striving to achieve.

Rewrite

Now that students have gotten their ideas down on paper, ask them to go over their drafts, looking for sentences that sound awkward, dialogue that sounds strained, and moments in the plot that lag or just don't make sense. Explain that in the rewrite stage, students are to fix their stories so they sound right to their own ears.

Proofread

Once students are pleased with their revisions, instruct them to proofread the story for punctuation, spelling, and grammar errors. You might allow students to exchange papers with partners and check each other's work.

Publish

Invite students to share their stories with the class. To save time, you might divide the class into small groups and encourage group members to read their stories to each other. Afterward, combine all the stories into your own science fiction/fantasy class magazine to keep in your reading center.

DESCRIBE YOUR NEW WORLD

Name _____ **Date** _____

To help organize your ideas, fill in the story web below.
Describe your new world in the center circle. In the surrounding
circles, describe the characters and any other important
elements of the setting.

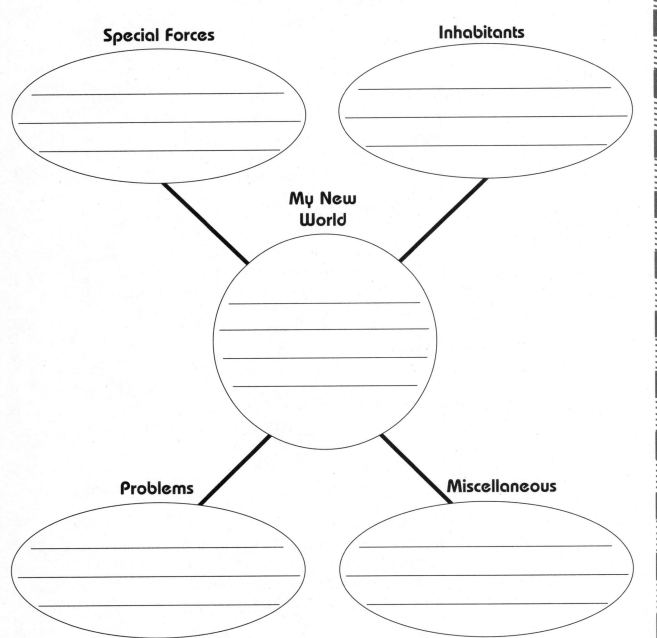

Special Forces

Inhabitants

My New World

Problems

Miscellaneous

More Writing Projects

Remind students that writing takes many forms. Encourage your students to try some of the writing projects suggested below.

- Prepare a poster depicting the climax of the story. Make sure you include the book title and author as well as a paragraph explaining the events.

- Create a travel brochure for this imaginary place. List places of interest for visitors to see as you describe the setting. Illustrate the brochure.

- Pretend the main character or another character from the story has been chosen Personality of the Month by a national magazine. Write a biographical sketch of the character, including his or her background and accomplishments.

- Is there another adventure that might happen in this magical, faraway place? Write a new story that takes place here. Perhaps the new story involves you as a main character.

Teacher Notes/Other _____

_____

_____

_____

_____

_____

_____

_____

_____

Bibliography

Titles that might be selected for this genre include, but are not limited to, the following.

The Castle in the Attic by Elizabeth Winthrop (Bantam, 1986).

The Dark Is Rising by Susan Cooper (Macmillan Books for Young Readers, 1986).

The Dollhouse Murders by Betty Ren Wright (Scholastic, Inc., 1985).

Eva by Peter Dickinson (Dell, 1990).

Greenwitch by Susan Cooper (Macmillan Books for Young Readers, 1986).

The Grey King by Susan Cooper (Macmillan Books for Young Readers, 1986).

The Hobbit by J.R.R. Tolkien (HM, 1989).

I, Houdini by Lynn Reid Banks (Avon, 1989).

Journey to the Center of the Earth by Jules Verne (Bantam, 1991).

Matilda by Roald Dahl (Puffin Books, 1990).

My Robot Buddy by Alfred Slote (HarperCollins Children's Books, 1986).

My Teacher Is an Alien by Bruce Coville (PB, 1990).

Omega Station by Alfred Slote (HarperCollins Children's Books, 1986).

Over Sea, Under Stone by Susan Cooper (Macmillan Books for Young Readers, 1989).

The Search for Delicious by Natalie Babbitt (Farrar, Straus, & Giroux, 1969).

Shoebag by Mary James (Scholastic, 1990).

Silver on the Tree by Susan Cooper (Macmillan Books for Young Readers, 1987).

Stinker from Space by Pamela F. Service (Fawcett, 1989).

The Trouble on Janus by Alfred Slote (HarperCollins Children's Books, 1988).

Under Alien Stars by Pamela F. Service (Fawcett, 1991).

Voices After Midnight by Richard Peck (Yearling Classics, 1990).

The Voyage Begun by Nancy Bond (Macmillan Books for Young Readers, 1981).

When the Dolls Woke by Marjorie Filley Stover (Scholastic, Inc., 1993).

The Wish Giver: Three Tales of Coven Tree by Bill Brittain (HarperCollins Children's Books, 1986).

INTRODUCING THE GENRE

Although some students may flinch at the idea of poetry, it is an ideal literary form for student study. Poetry pushes students to search for comprehension and work at the craft of writing. Many poems are loaded with literary techniques that can be applied to other types of writing. Poetry also comes in many different forms—even shapes. In fact, you might make the argument that poetry allows students to be their most creative—to freely express their thoughts in flowing lines that can rhyme, but don't have to, that can follow a pattern, but don't have to. Students' poems can be whatever they want. The key is to *make every word count.*

- Page 106 provides examples of different types of poetry for students to explore.

- The bibliography on page 114 suggests poetry anthologies by premier poets as well as various collections.

- Strategies for reading comprehension and poetry analysis can be found on pages 107–108.

- Writing activities begin on page 109.

Check Out These Poetic Styles

Before reading poetry, it may be wise to review with students some different poetic styles. Poems come in many forms. The forms your students choose to try can be suggested by you or left up to them. Here are some guidelines.

- **Rhyming Couplet:** simple verse in which the last words rhyme.

    I think it's great,
    That you can skate.

- **Quatrain:** a poem with four lines. The lines may all rhyme or rhyming lines may be offset.

    I think it's great,
    I think it's nice,
    That we can skate,
    Upon the ice.

- **Limerick:** silly five-line poems with a distinct pattern.

    I once knew a woman named Kate.
    Who decided she wanted to skate.
    She took off 'cross the ice,
    And she fell once, then twice,
    But we think that Katy skates great.

- **Cinquain:** five-line poems that are great for building vocabulary.

    Snow (subject, noun)
    Silent, silvery (two adjectives)
    Falling, whirling, floating (three verbs)
    Covering the street so white. (descriptive phrase)
    Winter (noun)

- **Haiku:** Japanese poetry style consisting of three lines with 5 syllables in the first line, 7 syllables in the second, and 5 in the third. Most haiku are about nature.

    Autumn leaves fall down.
    Billowy piles at my feet.
    I tumble in them.

- **Shape Poem:** format takes on the shape of its subject.

- **Free-form:** poems that don't necessarily rhyme or follow a strict pattern.

Name _____   Date _____

Title of Poem

_____

Poet: _____

What is this poem about? _____

_____

What type of poem, or what style, is it? _____

Does the poem rhyme? _____

How does the poem make you feel? _____

_____

List five descriptive words from the poem that really "work" for you. _____

_____

_____

What is your favorite line from the poem? _____

_____

_____

What other things does this poem make you think of? _____

_____

_____

Find two other poems written by this poet. Write the titles here.

1. _____

2. _____

What message do you think the poet is trying to get across? _____

_____

_____

POETRY DETAIL CHART

_____ _____
Name   Date

Think about the main idea of the poem. Write it in the first box. What details does the poet use to support or describe the main idea? Write the supporting details in the other boxes.

The Main Idea

Supporting Details

Journal Prompts

Encourage students to write in their journals about the poems they read. The following prompts will get them started. Point out to students that poetry can take on different styles. What kinds of poems might they like to write?

- Would you choose to write about the same subject as the poet? Why or why not?

- Think about what inspired the poet to write a poem on this subject. Explain the poet's choice from the poet's point of view.

- If you could add a line or two to the poem, what would you write? Write your new lines in your journal.

- Pretend that this poem is a song. Which contemporary singer would sing this poem? Explain your answer.

- Judging the poet by the style of the poem, what do you think the poet might be like? Write a personality sketch of the poet.

- Write a new title for the poem. Explain why you think it is appropriate.

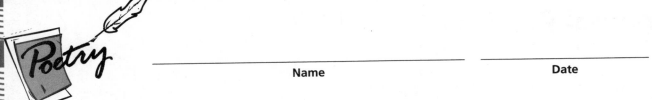

WRITE YOUR OWN POEM

_____   _____

Name   **Date**

Consider a subject you would like to write a poem about.
Remember, poetry doesn't have to be serious! Your poem can
be about something funny, about something everyday, about a
color, a feeling, a season, a friend, an animal—
anything! It's up to you.

Write your ideas below.

_____

_____

_____

_____

_____

When people read my poem, I would like them to feel _____ .

_____

_____

I would like to try to write this type of poetry: _____ .

_____

_____

Here are some poetic phrases that came into my head.

1. _____

2. _____

3. _____

4. _____

5. _____

The Writing Process

Guide students as they follow these steps in the writing process.

Prewrite

Poetry writing shouldn't be intimidating to students. Give them ample time to consider formats and ideas, perhaps setting up a free-flow thought period. Encourage students to plan their poems using the worksheet on page 110. For students who wish to come up with rhyming words, pass out the rhyming web on page 112. Students may also map out their poems using the Poetry Detail Chart on page 108.

Draft

Encourage students to combine their thoughts and ideas into poems. Remind students that their poems do not have to rhyme. As students write, suggest that they keep in mind the mood they wish their poems to evoke. How do they want readers to feel as they read this poem?

Rewrite

Have students set their poems aside to read later with fresh eyes. How do they like their poems the second time around? Are there words or phrases they would like to change? Are there new ideas they would like to add? Do they enjoy the flow and rhythm of their poems? Encourage students to make the changes they feel are needed.

Proofread

Have students read their poems one final time to make sure they have spelled all the words correctly and punctuated the lines properly. Allow students to exchange their poems with classmates to check for basic errors.

Publish

Arrange the class in a cozy circle so students can share their poems. Since poems are usually short, encourage the entire class to participate. If students feel awkward reading their own work, they may exchange poems with partners and read their partners' poems. Then create a class poetry anthology to keep in your reading center.

Poetry

Name _____ **Date** _____

Write the word you would like to rhyme in the center
circle. Then, as you think up rhyming words, write them in
the surrounding circles. Keep your rhyming-word
webs in your writing folder.

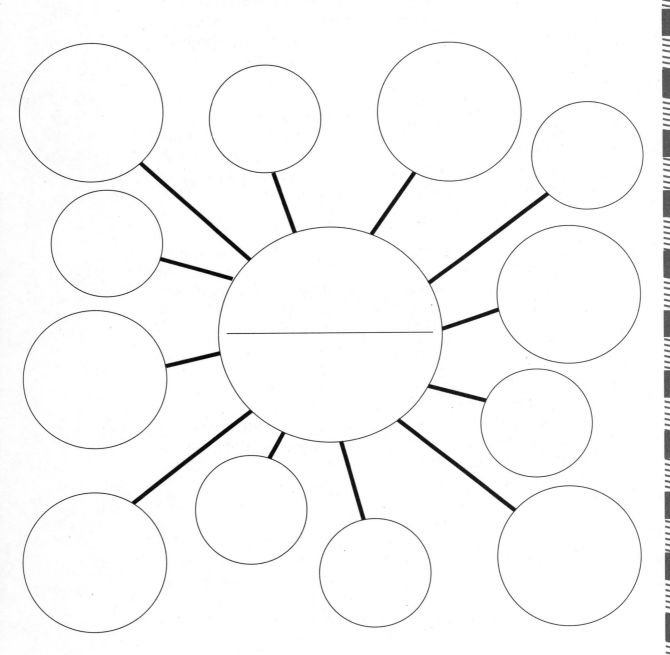

ore Writing Projects

Remind students that poetry has many forms. Encourage your students to stretch their poetry skills by trying the following.

- Think about a favorite sport or activity. Come up with a silly character who tries to master it. Write a limerick describing what happens.

- What is your favorite color? Write a cinquain to describe it.

- Take a walk outside. Write a haiku about your experience.

- Pretend your best friend has just been awarded a special prize. You wish to honor your friend with a poem. Write a poem, in any style, about your friend.

- Think about the things that happen at your house. Write a shape poem, in the shape of your home, to tell about them.

Teacher Notes/Other _____

_____

_____

_____

_____

_____

_____

_____

_____

_____

Bibliography

Many excellent poetry anthologies are available in your local bookstore and library. Even those for younger children can provide your students with fine models. Here are a few to check out.

Brats by X. J. Kennedy (Macmillan Books for Young Readers, 1986).

Fire in My Hands: A Book of Poems by Gary Soto (Scholastic, Inc., 1992).

For Laughing Out Loud: Poems to Tickle Your Funnybone, selected by Jack Prelutsky (Alfred A. Knopf Books for Young Readers, 1991).

Going Over to Your Place, selected by Paul B. Janeczko (Bradbury Press, 1987).

Good Books, Good Times! edited by Lee Bennet Hopkins (HarperCollins Children's Books, 1990).

Hailstones and Halibut Bones by Mary O'Neill (Doubleday, 1990).

Joyful Noise: Poems for Two Voices by Paul Fleischman (HarperCollins Children's Books, 1992).

Never Say Boo to a Ghost by John Foster (Scholastic, Inc., 1991).

The New Kid on the Block by Jack Prelutsky (Greenwillow Books, 1984).

The Random House Book of Poetry for Children, selected by Jack Prelutsky (Random House Books for Young Readers, 1983).

Reflections on a Gift of Watermelon Pickle & Other Modern Verse by Stephen Dunning, et. al. (Lothrop, Lee & Shepard Books, 1966).

Sing a Song of Popcorn, selected by Beatrice Schenk de Regniers, et al (Scholastic, Inc., 1988).

Something BIG Has Been Here by Jack Prelutsky (Greenwillow Books, 1990).

Spin a Soft Black Song by Nikki Giovanni (Farrar, Straus, & Giroux, 1985).

The D-Poems of Jeremy Bloom by Gordon and Bernice Korman (Scholastic, Inc., 1992).

Tyrannosaurus Was a Beast by Jack Prelutsky (William Morrow & Co., 1992).

You Come Too by Robert Frost (Henry Holt & Co., Inc., 1959).

Where the Sidewalk Ends: Poems & Drawings by Shel Silverstein (HarperCollins Children's Books, 1974).

Zoo Doings: Animal Poems by Jack Prelutsky (Greenwillow Books, 1983).

INTRODUCING THE GENRE

PLAYS

Let's put on a show! Writing and performing plays is a wonderful way not only to involve the whole class but also to get students to work cooperatively. Reading plays may be a new experience for your students. As they read plays you or they select, encourage them to notice the format. Dialogue is, of course, the most important component of a play. Everything we know about the characters and plot we must learn through the dialogue. Challenge students to notice other aspects as well. How is the setting described? How can we tell what the characters are feeling? Once students get the feel for the play format, they can begin to write and perform plays of their own.

- Page 116 provides summaries and a partial listing of plays from three play collections.

- On page 124 you will find a bibliography of play anthologies as well as other resources for putting on a show.

- Strategies for reading comprehension and story analysis can be found on pages 117–118.

- Writing activities start on page 119.

Check Out These Titles

The following three books contain plays that are fun to read with your students. You might choose one play and assign roles so the class may enjoy the play together. Or have students read the plays in small groups.

Plays Children Love edited by Coleman A. Jennings and Aurand Harris (Doubleday, 1981). This book is loaded with plays, many of which are based on popular children's stories.

- *Wiley and the Hairy Man* by Jack Stokes.
- *Ming Lee and the Magic Tree* by Aurand Harris.
- *Tom Sawyer* by Sara Spencer.

Plays of Black Americans edited by Sylvia E. Kamerman (Plays, Inc., 1987). For a historical turn, try these plays written about moments and people in African American history.

- *Harriet Tubman—the Second Moses* by Aileen Fisher.
- *Crispus Attucks* by Aileen Fisher.
- *George Washington Carver* by Mildred Hark and Noel McQueen.

Contemporary Children's Theater edited by Betty Jean Liften (Equinox Books/Avon, 1974). These plays are fun and exciting and deal with contemporary issues.

- *The Riddle Machine* by Beth Lambert.
- *Starman Jones* by Douglas L. Lieberman.
- *The Comical Tragedy or Tragical Comedy of Punch and Judy* by Aurand Harris.

PLAYS

_____   _____
Name   Date

Title of Play

_____

Playwright: _____

Who are the **main characters?** _____

_____

Where and when does the play take place? (**Setting**) _____

_____

What is the play about? (**Plot**) _____

_____

_____

What is the **mood** of the play? (For example, funny, serious, informational,

spooky.) _____

How many **acts** does the play have? _____

How many **scenes**? _____

List the **supporting characters.** _____

_____

Choose a **main character.** _____

Describe what he or she is like. _____

_____

_____

What happens at the **climax** of the play? _____

_____

_____

_____

PLAYS

_____   _____
Name   Date

Just like other stories in other genres, the action in a play builds to a climax. Complete the diagram below to chart the play's exposition, rising action, climax, falling action, and conclusion.

Climax

Rising Action

Falling Action

Exposition

Conclusion

Journal Prompts

Invite students to record in their journals any thoughts, comments, and ideas they have about the plays they read. Encourage students to think about plays they might like to write.

- List the characters in your play and note the different personalities of each.

- If you were an actor, which role would you like to play? Choose a character and explain why you would like to play him or her.

- Write a new character for the play—a character that you would like to perform yourself. What would the character be like? Write a few lines for the character to say.

- Pretend this play was set in a different setting or time period. Do you think the characters would act the same way? Create a new setting and rewrite one scene in the new setting.

- Suppose that this play was produced on Broadway. Do you think you would have enjoyed it? Write a review of the play.

- Imagine that this play is a musical. What songs would you write for it? Give the titles of at least three songs you would add. Which character would sing them? Try writing the lyrics for one.

PLAYS

Name _____   Date _____

Think about an incident that would make a good play. It can be something that really happened, something you read in a book, or something you create.

Write a scene for a play based on your incident.

Title _____

Main character _____

Main character's personality _____

_____

Another main character _____

This character's personality _____

_____

Setting (time and place) _____

General plot _____

_____

_____

_____

Supporting characters _____

_____

This play will be a comedy/drama/mystery/melodrama. (Circle one.)

What I would like people to get from this play _____

_____

_____

_____

120

The Writing Process

Guide students as they follow these steps in the writing process.

Prewrite

It is important to outline the action of a play. Suggest that students record their ideas on the worksheet on page 120. Then ask them to consider the action, mapping it on the worksheet on page 118. Have students write ideas for dialogue on the worksheet on page 122. Another fun way for students to prepare for playwriting is to collect *overheard dialogue.* Encourage students to keep a pocket notebook and write down interesting conversations they overhear at home, at the mall, or at school. Portions of these real conversations may be used in their plays.

Draft

Students may wish to refer to published plays for style and format. Suggest that students put themselves into the action of the play as they write their first draft. This may help the dialogue and ideas flow more freely and naturally. Tell students not to worry about stage directions yet but to concentrate on the overall flow of the play and conversations of the characters.

Rewrite

As students reread their plays, tell them to think about how their characters move. Will they cross the stage? Shake someone's hand? Sit down? Run off? Will their faces convey certain emotions? Have students add stage directions that explain the actors' movements. Encourage partners to read their plays aloud to each other.

Proofread

Ask students to read for spelling, grammar, and punctuation. Encourage students to check dictionaries and grammar books and make the appropriate corrections.

Publish

Divide the class into groups and encourage groups to assign roles and read each other's plays. Then ask groups to choose one play to perform or read through for the class. Performances need not be elaborate.

Name _____ Date _____

As you ponder your play, lines of dialogue may occur to you.
You don't want to forget them! Fill in dialogue that you could
use in your play in the speech bubbles below.

Main Character

Main Character

Supporting Character

Supporting Character

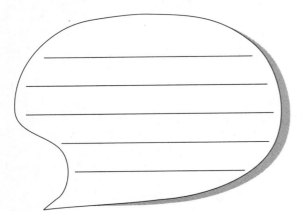

More Writing Projects

Remind students that writing takes many forms. Encourage your students to try some of the writing projects suggested below.

- Your play has just opened on Broadway. Write a newspaper review about it. Be objective! Which parts were excellent? Which parts needed work? (You might also review the published play you read.)

- The lead actor in your play has won an award for a stellar performance. Write an acceptance speech for your actor to deliver at an awards ceremony.

- A CD of the musical score of your play has just been released. Write the copy that would go on the album cover.

- Design a poster to advertise your play. Make sure it captures the mood of your play and lists the actors. You may wish to include excerpts from your review.

Teacher Notes/Other _____

_____

_____

_____

_____

_____

_____

_____

_____

_____

Bibliography

Check out these titles to enhance students' appreciation of plays. The starred entries are anthologies.

Christmas Play Favorites for Young People by Sylvia E. Kamerman (Plays, Inc, 1982).

Contemporary Children's Theater edited by Betty Jean Liften (Equinox Books/Avon, 1974).

Folk Tale Plays for Puppets by Lewis Mahlmann and David Cadwalader Jones (Plays, Inc., 1980).

It's Time to Give a Play by Janette Woolsey and Elizabeth Hough Sechrist (Macrae Smith, 1955).

Making Costumes for School Plays by Joan Peters and Anna Sutcliffe. (Plays, Inc., 1987).

Plays Children Love edited by Coleman A. Jennings and Aurand Harris (Doubleday, 1981).

Plays for Modern Teen-age Actors by Harold Cable (Plays, Inc., 1971).

Plays of Black Americans. Edited by Sylvia E. Kamerman (Plays, Inc., 1987).

Plays—The Drama Magazine for Young People (Plays, Inc.)

Puppet Shows: Using Poems and Stories by Laura Ross (Lothrop, Lee & Shepard, 1970).

Putting on a Play by Nick Pryor (Thomas Learning, 1994).

Stage Plays from the Classics by Joellen Bland (Plays, Inc., 1987).

Staging a School Play by Peter Chilver (Harper, 1967).

Theater Magic: Behind the Scenes at a Children's Theater by Cheryl Walsh Bellville (Carolrhoda Books, 1986).

READING ASSESSMENT

Student's Name		Date		

Behaviors and Attitudes	rarely	occasionally	frequently
Completes assignments with care			
Sustains reading for at least 20 minutes			
Writes effective responses to literature			
Participates and shares during sharing sessions			
Listens to and enjoys read-aloud books			
Reads a variety of genres			
Strategies			
Knows how to select appropriate reading material			
Knows when and why to abandon reading material			
Takes risks: predicting, discussing, pronouncing			
Keeps a log of books read, with comments			
Reads fluently			
Connects reading materials to own life			
Connects reading materials to other books			
Refers back to text to support statements			
When encountering an unfamiliar word, knows when to • skip and go on • self-correct • supply a meaningful substitute			
Makes inferences (reads between the lines)			
Compares characters			
Retells main points in an organized fashion			
Identifies point of view			
Engages in self-evaluation			
Enjoyment/Involvement			
Is aware of a variety of reading materials and can select those he or she enjoys			
Responds with emotion to text: laughs, cries, smiles			
Can get "lost" in a book			
Chooses to read during free time			
Wants to continue reading when time is up			
Has books on hand to read			
Can identify the work of authors he or she enjoys			
Sees literature as a way of knowing about the world			

Self-Evaluation ☐   Teacher Evaluation ☐   (NE = Not evaluated at this time)

WRITING ASSESSMENT

Student's Name _____ Date _____

Ideas and Content	Seldom	Sometimes	Frequently	Always
Writes with obvious purpose				
Chooses relevant titles				
Supports main idea with details				
Demonstrates high-quality work				
Demonstrates originality and creativity				
Style and Vocabulary				
Varies word choice				
Attempts to vary sentence beginnings				
Attempts to use a variety of sentence types				
Organization and Paragraph Development				
Sequences paragraphs logically				
Usually uses appropriate paragraph development				
Provides appropriate introduction and conclusion				
Usually uses a new paragraph for each new idea				
Develops story line appropriately				
Spelling and Mechanics				
Spells common words correctly				
Uses all words in recognizable context				
Uses appropriate capitalization and indentation				
Uses appropriate punctuation				
Grammar, Usage, and Sentence Structure				
Uses correct verb tense				
Generally uses standard English				
Generally uses correct subject/verb agreement				
Omits few words				
Uses few sentence fragments or run-ons				
Handwriting and Appearance				
Demonstrates overall neat appearance (correct margins, heading, and title)				
Uses consistent letter formation (size, slant, and spacing)				

Self-Evaluation ☐   Teacher Evaluation ☐   (NE = Not evaluated at this time)

COMPREHENSION CHECK

Student's Name _____

1 Book: _____ Genre: _____

Comments: Date: _____

Words to review:

2 Book: _____ Genre: _____

Comments: Date: _____

Words to review:

3 Book: _____ Genre: _____

Comments: Date: _____

Words to review:

4 Book: _____ Genre: _____

Comments: Date: _____

Words to review:

	1	2	3	4
Makes predictions about story				
Participates in discussion				
Answers questions on all levels				
Determines word meaning through context				
Reads smoothly and fluently				
Can retell selection using own words				
Comprehends after silent reading				
Can "read between the lines"				
Possesses broad background knowledge				

Key

Often +   Seldom −

Sometimes S   Not Observed N

Based on Wood's Group Comprehension Matrix

READING QUESTIONNAIRE

_____   _____
Name   **Date**

1. Do you like to read? _____ Why? _____

_____

2. What kinds of books do you like to read or listen to? _____

_____

3. The *best* book I ever read was _____

4. What do you do when you are reading and come to something you don't

   know? _____

_____

5. Do you think reading is important? _____ Why? _____

_____

_____

6. Do you go to another library besides the school library? _____

   Which one? _____ How often? _____

7. Is reading hard or easy for you? _____ Why? _____

_____

_____

8. I read books at home ☐   at school ☐.

9. What is your favorite subject in school? _____

   Why? _____

_____

10. What do you like to do in your spare time? _____

_____

_____

11. **Are you a good reader?** _____ **Why?** _____

_____

_____

12. **I enjoy reading because** _____

_____

_____

13. **Sometimes I don't like to read when** _____

_____

_____

14. **Are you a good writer?** _____ **Why?** _____

_____

_____

15. **I enjoy writing because** _____

_____

_____

16. **Sometimes I don't like writing when** _____

_____

_____

17. **What languages do you or your family speak at home?** _____

_____

18. **Is your family a family of readers?** _____

19. **Is there time and a place for you to read at home?** _____

20. **What is the most important thing you need to do to become a better reader?**

_____

_____

_____

Name _____   Date _____

Book Title

_____

Word	Page Number	Meaning

Name _____ Date _____

Book Title

_____

Word	Synonym	Antonym
stuffy	stifling	comfortable

_____   _____

Name   Date

Write a word in the middle circle. Fill in the outer circles with words that have similar meanings.

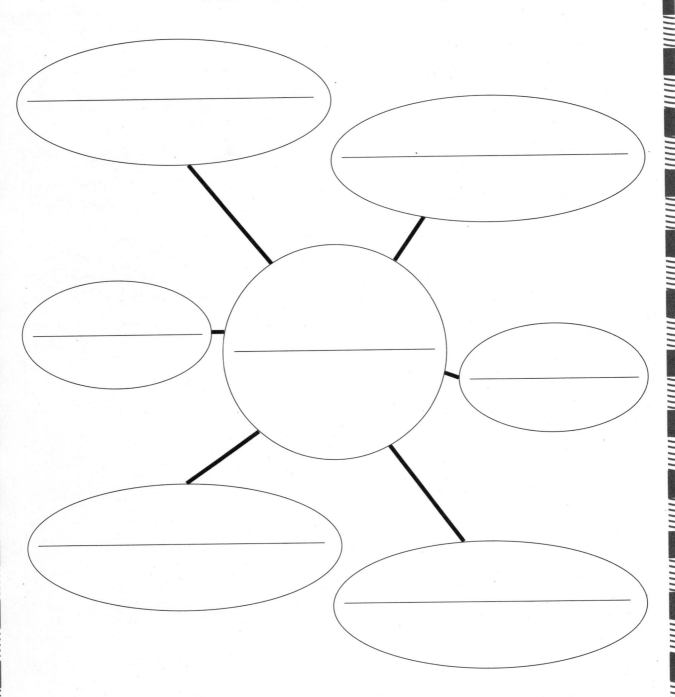

Adjective: a word that modifies a noun

Adverb: a word that modifies a verb

Consider making a word cube for both adjectives and adverbs.

For extra credit, you may make as many word cubes as you like

Select six adverbs or adjectives the author uses to set the action of the story. Carefully print one word on each square above. Cut out the cube. Fold along the solid lines to form the cube and spread glue on the shaded tabs. Slip the tabs inside the cube and attach firmly. Let dry.

When you meet in your discussion groups, use the cubes to trade words and moods. Toss your cube to another student. Challenge him or her to pronounce the word, tell whether it is an adverb or adjective, and give an example of a noun or verb it might modify or describe. The student may then toss his or her own cube to another player to continue the game.

Extra: Make a vocabulary cube of new nouns from your story.

Bloom's Taxonomy

Bloom's Taxonomy delineates six progressively more advanced levels of critical thinking. The levels are listed below, along with verbs and phrases that suggest appropriate activities for each level. For example, a science task at the *application* level might ask a student to *illustrate* the water cycle. When questioning students or creating assignments at the middle-school level, be sure to go beyond the knowledge and comprehension levels in order to stretch and challenge students' critical thinking abilities.

Knowledge
tell, list, name, repeat, remember, recall, match, locate

Comprehension
explain, find, define, illustrate, diagram, summarize, restate, describe

Application
solve, use, demonstrate, illustrate, show, report, classify, put in order, apply, report

Analysis
examine, survey, compare, contrast, alike/different, separate, chart, advertise, distinguish

Synthesis
create, invent, imagine, compose, pretend, predict, plan, improve, what if, modify

Evaluation
judge, select, choose, decide, debate, write a letter, hold a court trial, what is the best way, what could have been different, evaluate, verify, argue

Using these critical-thinking principles not only helps students enhance their comprehension but also provides a useful guide for evaluation. The following list suggests alternative questions one might use to develop new study guides or modify old ones.

Reading Questions for Study Guides

Knowledge

- Tell the who, what, when, where and why of the story.
- List the main characters in your play and explain their role in the play.
- List five major events in the story in chronological order.
- List the main characters in your book.
- List five significant events from the person's life you read about. List them in the order in which they occurred.
- Who is telling this story? (point of view)
- Identify the main characters in a crossword puzzle.
- Match statements with the character who said them.
- List the main characteristics of the main characters in "Wanted" posters.
- Arrange scrambled story sentences in sequential order.
- Recall details about the setting by creating a picture of where the story took place.
- Which historical character or what historical event is the focus of this book?

Comprehension

- Write a short (one page) summary of the plot.
- Who was your favorite character in the play? _____ Write a paragraph describing him or her and list the pages where you found that information.
- Find five adjectives in the story that helped create the mood.
- Write a short summary of the person's life and explain the specific reasons this person is remembered.
- Write a short (one page) summary of the plot of your book.
- Explain selected ideas or parts from the story in your own words.
- Draw a picture showing what happened before and after a passage or illustration found in the book.
- Write a sentence explaining what happened before and after a passage or illustration found in the book.

- Predict what could happen next in the story before the reading of the entire book is completed.
- Construct a pictorial time line that summarizes what happens in the story.
- Explain how the main character felt at the beginning, middle, and/or end of the story.
- Describe the time and setting of this story.

Application

- Pretend one of the animals in the story is lost. Write a descriptive lost and found item for a newspaper.
- Put the plot into six sequential sentences.
- Write an advertisement to entice someone else to read the book.
- Pretend you are the person you read about. Write a diary entry during a special time in "your" life.
- Using adding machine tape (get from the teacher) create a time line for this story. Make sure events appear in the correct sequence. Illustrate as appropriate.
- Classify the characters as human, animal, or inanimate.
- Transfer a main character to a new setting.
- Select a meal that one of the main characters would enjoy eating, plan a menu, and a method for serving.
- Think of a situation that occurred to a character in the story and write about how you would have handled the situation differently.
- Give examples of people you know who have the same problems as the characters in the story.
- Using the information from the book, write five head-lines that could be used in a history book.
- Draw a time line showing the main events in the story in the order in which they happened. Relate these events to the actual world events. Use the encyclopedia to verify accurate dates of the real events.

Analysis

- Would you want the animal in this story for a pet? Explain why or why not.

- Would you want the person in this story for a friend? Explain why or why not.
- Why was the character you picked in # 2 important to the play?
- Would the main character make a good friend? Tell why or why not.
- Analyze the author's style. Tell what techniques she or he used to capture and hold your attention.
- Identify general characteristics (stated and/or implied) of the main characters.
- Distinguish what could happen from what could not have happened in the story in real life.
- Select parts of the story that were funniest, saddest, happiest, and most unbelievable.
- Differentiate fact from opinion.
- Compare and/or contrast two of the main characters.
- Select an action of a main character that was exactly the same as something you would have done.
- Describe the impact or role this character and/or event has had on society.

Synthesis

- Pretend another animal is going to be added to the story. Tell the kind of animal to be added and what role it is to play in the story.
- Create a new character and tell how that character would fit into the story.
- Write at least three questions you would ask the character you created if she or he were a real person.
- Write a new ending for the story.
- Prepare a list of five or more questions you would like to ask the person you have been reading about if you could have a chance to sit down and talk with him or her.
- Create a story from just the title before reading the story.
- Write three new titles for the story that would give a good idea of what it was about.
- Create a new product related to the story.
- Restructure the roles of the main characters to create new outcomes in the story.

- Compose and perform a dialogue or monologue that will communicate the thoughts of the main character at a given point in the story.
- Imagine that you are one of the main characters. Write a diary account of your daily thoughts and activities.
- Write the lyrics and music for a song that one of the main characters would sing if she or he became a rock star. Perform it.
- Choose one of the human conflicts in the story and write a change in the event that would alter the course of history.

Evaluation

- List three reasons you do or do not enjoy reading animal stories. Explain.
- Did you like or dislike this play? Explain your answer in two or three complete sentences.
- Did you like or dislike this story? Explain your answer.
- Do you think a biography/autobiography should have been written about this person? Explain in detail why you do or do not. You may want to cite specific happenings in the book by page number.
- What is your criteria for judging a good book? Using your criteria, how would you evaluate this book?
- Decide which character in the story you would most like to spend a day with. Why?
- Judge whether or not a character should have acted in a particular way and explain why.
- Decide if the story really could have happened and give reasons for your decision.
- Consider how this story can help you in your own life.
- Appraise the value of the story.
- Compare the story with another one you have read.
- Write a recommendation as to why the book should or should not be read.
- Write a newspaper or television review of the book stating your opinions regarding the overall quality of the story.

Reading Conference Questions

Questions such as the ones below may be used as you confer with individual children, a small group of students, or as the basis for student discussions in sharing groups. **Boldface** topics indicate areas that are explored by each group of questions.

Author

Why do you suppose the author chose this title?

What is the main thing the author is saying to you?

If you had a chance to talk with this author, what would you talk about?

What other books by this author have you read? How are the other books like this one?

What do you know about the author? How can you tell?

What is the author trying to tell you in your book?

What did the author have to know to write this book?

What sorts of things does the author like or dislike?

If the author asked you what could be improved in this story, what would you say?

Characters

Would you like to be one of the people in this story? Who? Why?

Did any of the characters remind you of people you know? Explain.

Which character interested you the most? Is he or she the most important person in the story? Discuss.

Which character(s) didn't you like? Why?

Who are the main characters in your story? Do you like or dislike them? Why?

Choose one character. Why is this character important in the story?

Do any of the characters change? In what way?

Do any of the characters do things that you think are good? Wrong?

Choosing Books

I see you're reading _____. What do you think of it?

What makes this a good book for you?

How did you decide to read this?

Is there anybody else in our class you think would enjoy reading this? Why?

What is the best book you read this quarter? What makes it the best?

Comprehension

Do you have any confusion about what you've read?

What have you been wondering about as you read this?

What kind of "think-alouds" have you done as you read this book?

Goals

What would you like to do to become a better reader?

What do you have to do in order to be a good reader?

What do you want to do as a reader in the next nine weeks?

Illustrations

Who is the illustrator?

Do you like the illustrations? Why? Why not?

What (if anything) did the illustrations add to the text?

If the illustrations were not there, would there need to be more words? Why?

What do you think the illustrator needed to know in order to illustrate this story?

Journal

Why did you write _____ in your reading journal? Explain it to me.

Mood

How did you feel while reading the book? Why did you feel that way?

What was the funniest part? Saddest?

What was the most exciting or strangest thing that happened?

What do you remember most about the story?

Plot

Does this remind you of other books you have read?

Are there parts of this story that you have especially liked or disliked?

Tell me the main things that happened in your story.

Were you able to guess what was going to happen at the end?

Can you think of another way your story might have happened or ended?

Point of View

Did you feel as if everything was happening to you, as if you were one of the characters in the book? Or did you feel as if you were an observer, watching what was happening but not part of the action?

If you were an observer, where were you watching from? Was it from different places—sometimes from beside the characters, sometimes from above them as if in a helicopter? Can you tell me places in the book where you felt like that?

Read Aloud

What part of this book is special to you in some way? Read it to me.

Where did you leave off? Read to me from that place.

Setting

Where does the story take place? Tell me what the place was like.

Have you ever been to a place like this?

Did it matter where the story happened or could it have happened anywhere? Do you remember thinking about the place as you were reading?

Did the story take place a long time ago/in the future/now?

Style

What special words does the author use to help you "hear" or "see" in the story?

Tell me about any pictures the author has left in your mind.

What do you like about the way the author has written the story?

Theme

Why do you think the author wrote this book?

Do you think there is a message in this story? What is it?

What is the embedded theme?

Vocabulary

What strategy helps you most when you come to a word you don't know?

_____   _____
Name   **Date**

Independent Study

Book Titles
Respond to the following questions in complete sentences and paragraphs. Use another paper if there is not enough room on this page. The letters are supplied as hints to use Bloom's Taxonomy.

1. (K) Who is telling the story in each book? (point of view)

_____

_____

2. (C) Do you find a common purpose your author had in writing each of these books? Give examples (including page numbers) that support your answer.

_____

_____

3. (AN) Analyze the author's style in these books. How are both books similar? Tell what techniques she or he used to capture and hold your attention.

_____

_____

4. (E) Begin a letter to the author on the lines below. Tell the author what you like about his or her work. Also express any questions you had or confusion you felt. Use the back of the paper.

_____

_____

_____

_____

_____   _____
Name   Date

Discussion Group

Names in Group _____

_____

Date _____ **Author** _____

What common theme do you find in all of the books written by this author?

_____

_____

_____

What similarities do you find as you compare the main characters in each of the

different books that people in your group have read? _____

_____

_____

_____

_____

_____

Are there any similarities among the settings described in each of the books that

people in your group have read? List them here. _____

_____

_____

_____

_____

_____

_____

_____

Newbery Medal Winners (continued from page 34)

Title	Author	Year
The Story of Mankind	Hendrik Willem Van Loon	1922
The Voyages of Dr. Doolittle	Hugh Lofting	1923
The Dark Frigate	Charles Boardman Hawes	1924
Tales from Silver Lands	Charles J. Finger	1925
Shen of the Sea	Arthur Bowie Chrisman	1926
Smokey the Cow Horse	Will James	1927
Gay-Neck, The Story of a Pig	Dhan Gopal Mukerji	1928
The Trumpeter of Krakow	Eric P. Kelly	1929
Hitty: Her First Hundred Years	Rachel Field	1930
The Cat Who Went to Heaven	Elizabeth Coatsworth	1931
Waterless Mountain	Laura Adams Armer	1932
Young Fu of the Upper Yangtze	Elizabeth Foreman Lewis	1933
Invincible Louisa	Cornelia Meigs	1934
Dobry	Monica Shannon	1935
Caddie Woodlawn	Carol Ryrie Brink	1936
Roller Skates	Ruth Sawyer	1937
The White Stag	Kate Seredy	1938
Thimble Summer	Elizabeth Enright	1939
Daniel Boone	James Daugherty	1940
Call It Courage	Armstrong Sperry	1941
The Matchlock Gun	Walter Edmonds	1942
Adam of the Road	Elizabeth Janet Gray	1943
Johnny Tremain	Esther Forbes	1944
Rabbit Hill	Robert Lawson	1945
Strawberry Girl	Lois Lenski	1946
Miss Hickory	Carolyn Sherwin Bailey	1947
The 21 Balloons	William Pene Du Bois	1948
King of the Wind	Marguerite Henry	1949
The Door in the Wall	Marguerite De Angeli	1950
Amos Fortune: Free Man	Elizabeth Yates	1951
Ginger Pye	Eleanor Estes	1952
Secret of the Andes	Ann Nolan Clark	1953
... and Now Miguel	Joseph Krumgold	1954
The Wheel on the School	Meindert De Jong	1955
Carry On, Mr. Bowditch	Jean Lee Latham	1956
Miracles on Maple Hill	Virginia Sorensen	1957
Rifles for Watie	Harold Keith	1958
The Witch of Blackbird Pond	Elizabeth George Speare	1959
Onion John	Joseph Krumgold	1960
Island of the Blue Dolphins	Scott O'Dell	1961

Bibliography (continued from page 74)

Shh! We're Writing the Constitution by Jean Fritz (Putnam Publishing Group, 1987).

Space Garbage by Isaac Asimov (Dell, 1991).

Tales Mummies Tell by Patricia Lauber (HarperCollins Children's Books, 1985).

They Led the Way: Fourteen American Women by Johanna Johnston (Scholastic, Inc., 1987).

Undying Glory: The Story of the Massachusetts Fifty-Fourth Regiment by Clinton Cox (Scholastic, Inc., 1993).

Unidentified Flying Objects by Isaac Asimov (Dell, 1990).

Vikings by Robert Nicholson (Chelsea House, 1994).

Voyagers from Space: Meteors & Meteorites by Patricia Lauber (HarperCollins Children's Books, 1989).